POWERED BY
THE SUN

2007
SOLAR DECATHLON

THE NATIONAL MALL
WASHINGTON, D.C.
OCTOBER 12–20, 2007
www.solardecathlon.org

Photo Credits

Vertical column, top: The Cal Poly 2005 Solar Decathlon house frames a view of the U.S. Capitol. Bottom: The University of Colorado team, champion of the 2005 Solar Decathlon, celebrates with a victory lap in their electric vehicle. The remaining photos show 2007 Solar Decathlon teams planning and constructing their houses: New York Institute of Technology, University of Illinois at Urbana-Champaign, University of Cincinnati, and Penn State (note the OSHA-approved, cowboy-style hard hats).

With excitement running high, Secretary of Energy Samuel Bodman cuts the ribbon to open the 2005 Solar Decathlon. Looking on are sponsor representatives and students and faculty from the competing teams. Credit: Stefano Paltera

MESSAGE FROM THE SECRETARY OF ENERGY

Welcome to Washington, D.C., home of the nation's capital and the U.S. Department of Energy's third Solar Decathlon, a unique competition in which 20 college- and university-led teams from around the world work to design, finance, construct, and operate the most energy-efficient, solar-powered homes imaginable. These students have created living laboratories, where concept truly meets reality. And now their work will be put to the test.

Teams will be evaluated in 10 areas encompassing architecture, engineering, livability, comfort, space heating and cooling, water heating, and powering lights and appliances — representing the next generation of solar-powered homes and the promise of solar technology.

I want to congratulate all of the teams who are competing this year. With events such as the Solar Decathlon, not only are students working toward the goals outlined in President Bush's Solar America Initiative — which seeks to make solar energy cost competitive with conventional forms of electricity by 2015 — but they are also helping to make today's solar technology part of tomorrow's energy reality. Events such as this also bring to life the President's American Competitiveness Initiative, which aims to invest in our next generation of scientists, engineers, and educators to keep America at the forefront of science and innovation. Witnessing the work of this generation's best and brightest, you recognize that America's entrepreneurial spirit and passion for scientific discovery remain strong.

Whether you are here as a competitor, team supporter, or visitor, I hope you take the time to fully examine the breadth of cutting-edge technologies used in the solar village, some of which are available for use in your home today. Through projects such as the Solar Decathlon, we are developing clean technologies that can fundamentally change the way we power our homes and businesses.

Again, welcome, and enjoy the Solar Decathlon.

Samuel W. Bodman
U.S. Secretary of Energy

COMPETITION PROGRAM

Contents

WELCOME TO THE SOLAR DECATHLON

As you visit the Solar Decathlon, don't hold back on the oohs and aahs. Pointing and gesturing are okay, too. We think you'll be impressed and inspired as you tour the houses in the "solar village" and meet the student competitors on the National Mall.

The solar village comes to life for only a short time, which is October 12 through 20, 2007. But what an amazing village it is, complete with elegant, comfortable homes that operate solely on power from the sun.

These houses may seem futuristic, but they are based on materials and technologies that are available today. These houses were conceived, designed, engineered, and built primarily by students. Twenty teams of students from colleges and universities from the United States, including Puerto Rico; Canada; Germany; and Spain have come to compete. They have spent the past two years learning about the latest solar energy and energy efficiency technologies — and applying that knowledge to designing and building their own high-style, high-performance houses.

The teams built the houses on their home campuses and have transported them to the National Mall. Ten contests challenge their abilities to produce electricity and hot water from solar panels to perform all the functions of home — from turning on the lights to cooking, washing clothes and dishes, powering home electronics, and maintaining a comfortable temperature. The architectural style and livability of the homes are paramount.

Like Olympic decathletes, the "Solar Decathletes" draw on all of their strengths. Future engineers work with future architects to create energy-efficient homes that are also beautiful. They strive to innovate, using high-tech materials and design elements in ingenious ways.

Step into the Future

Visitors are important to the life of any village, but particularly so to the solar village. Sharing their hard-earned knowledge with the public is a key reason the students are here. They are passionate about their role in creating a new-energy future — a future that looks to be both environmentally sensible and economically secure.

So tour the houses and meet the students. Keep in mind that the Solar Decathlon is an intriguing competition. Formulating and executing a sound strategy is critically important. During house tours, you may want to ask the students about their overall strategy or strategy for a specific aspect of the competition that you find particularly interesting.

The team from the University of Colorado, the overall winner of both previous Solar Decathlons in 2002 and 2005, is back. Can Colorado win again, or will another team step up to the challenge and claim the trophy? Whatever happens, the competition is bound to be intense and compelling.

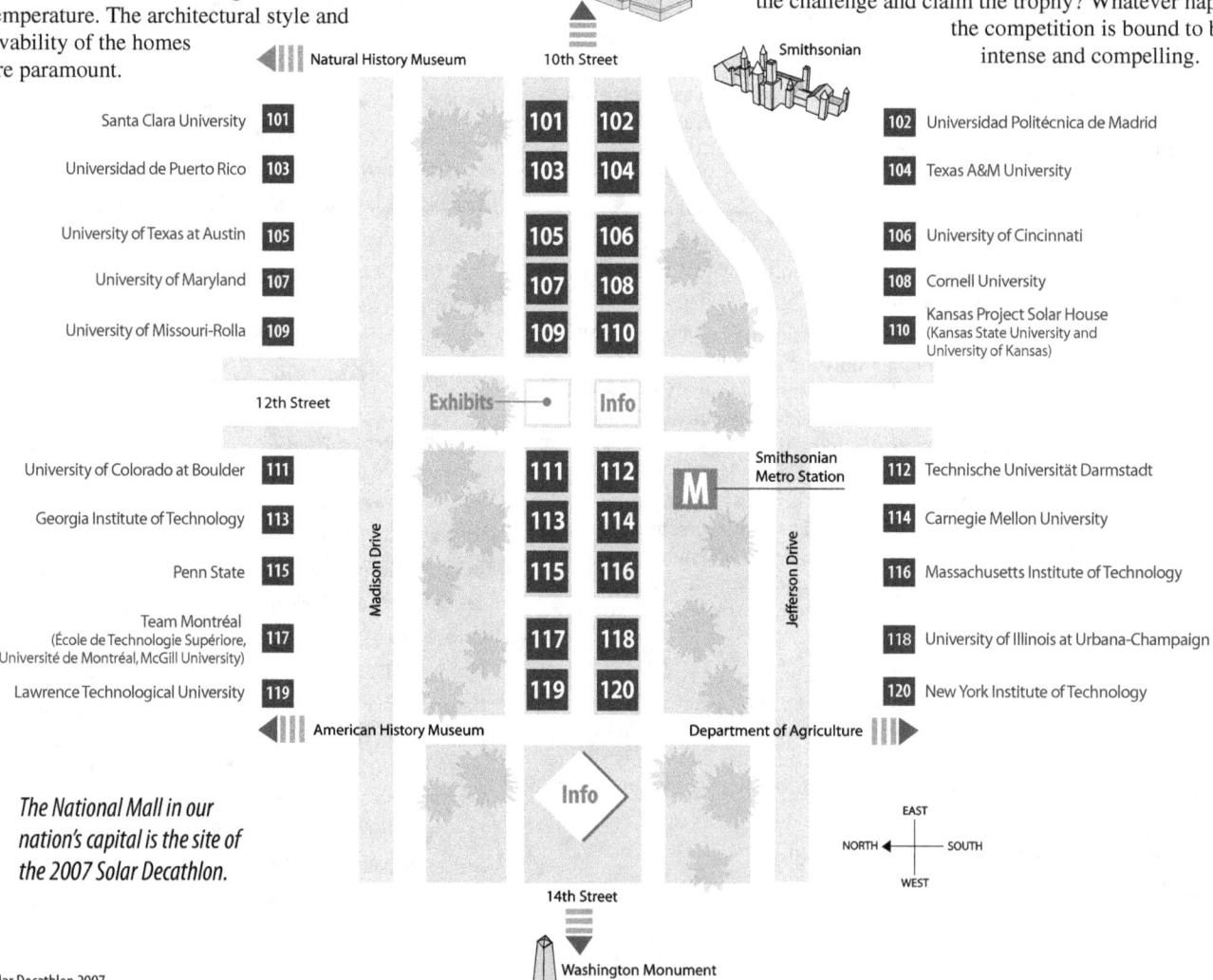

The National Mall in our nation's capital is the site of the 2007 Solar Decathlon.

THINGS TO SEE AND DO

Attend the Ceremonies

The Solar Decathlon Opening Ceremony is at 10:00 a.m., Friday, October 12. The Awards Ceremony is at 2:00 p.m., Friday, October 19, at which time the overall winner of the Solar Decathlon is announced. We encourage you to join in the excitement and cheer for your favorite team!

Tour the Team Houses

October 12–16 and October 18–20, 2007
11:00 a.m.–3:00 p.m., Weekdays; 10:00 a.m.–5:00 p.m., Weekends

The Solar Decathlon teams are here to compete. They're also here to share with you what they have learned. Team houses are living demonstrations of the latest in energy efficiency and renewable energy designs and products, and the best in home design.

On October 17, all houses are closed for competition purposes, but workshops are offered, and educational exhibits are open. Please note that during some public tour hours, some of the team houses are closed for competition purposes.

Visit the Educational Exhibits

October 12–20, 2007
11:00 a.m.– 3:00 p.m., Weekdays; 10:00 a.m.– 5:00 p.m., Weekends

Anatomy of a House

Located between the University of Missouri-Rolla (109) and University of Colorado (111) houses, this exhibit provides tips on saving energy for homeowners and includes several interactive features. The exhibit includes demonstrations of several building technologies used in the competition houses, as well as a depiction of a grid-connected photovoltaic (PV) system showing how a PV system would be set up for an average home. Unlike typical PV-powered houses, none of the Solar Decathlon houses are connected to the utility grid.

Powered by Renewables

The entire Solar Decathlon is powered by renewable energy during the event — this includes the team houses and all of the tents and trailers you see. Visit the exhibit (which is located in two places, near the two information tents) to see the PV systems and biodiesel generator powering the village.

Attend a Workshop

A variety of workshops will be held throughout the competition. So whatever your interest and expertise level, there is likely to be a session that suits your needs. And, as is true of the entire event, all workshops are free

For Consumers

October 13–17 and 20, 2007

Ask the Experts
Weekends only: 11:00 a.m.–1:00 p.m. and 3:30–5:30 p.m.
A group of green-building experts, coordinated by sponsor Blue Egg, will be on hand to answer questions.

Saturday, October 13

10:00 a.m.	DOE, *Energy Efficiency for the Homeowner*
11:30 a.m.	DOE, *Solar for the Homeowner*
1:00 p.m.	AIA, *AIA COTE Top Ten: A Focus on Top-Notch Design*
2:30 p.m.	DOE, *Energy Efficiency for the Homeowner*
4:00 p.m.	DOE, *Solar for the Homeowner*

Sunday, October 14

10:00 a.m.	DOE, *Energy Efficiency for the Homeowner*
11:30 a.m.	DOE, *Solar for the Homeowner*
1:00 p.m.	PATH, *Renovating Green and a 5-Year Green Plan*
2:30 p.m.	DOE, *Energy Efficiency for the Homeowner*
4:00 p.m.	DOE, *Solar for the Homeowner*

Monday, October 15

10:00 a.m.	PATH, *Renovating Green and a 5-Year Green Plan*
11:30 a.m.	DOE, *Energy Efficiency for the Homeowner*
1:00 p.m.	DOE, *Solar for the Homeowner*
2:30 p.m.	HON, *Empowering You: Environmental Solutions for Office Interiors*

Tuesday, October 16

10:00 a.m.	HON, *Empowering You: Environmental Solutions for Office Interiors*
11:30 a.m.	DOE, *Energy Efficiency for the Homeowner*
1:00 p.m.	DOE, *Solar for the Homeowner*
2:30 p.m.	Sprint, *Solar Energy*

Wednesday, October 17

10:00 a.m.	DOE, *Solar Best Practices for Homeowners*
11:30 a.m.	ASHRAE, *Solar Applications for the Homeowner*
1:00 p.m.	Texas Instruments, *Solar Dodecahedron — Scaling up the Solar Decathlon*
2:30 p.m.	Sprint, *Solar Energy*

Saturday, October 20

10:00 a.m.	DOE, *Energy Efficiency for the Homeowner*
11:30 a.m.	DOE, *Solar for the Homeowner*
1:00 p.m.	PATH, *Renovating Green and a 5-Year Green Plan*
2:30 p.m.	DOE, *Energy Efficiency for the Homeowner*
4:00 p.m.	DOE, *Solar for the Homeowner*

Building Industry Day

A special day devoted to building industry professionals.
Thursday, October 18, 2007

Ask the Experts: 9:00 a.m.–5:00 p.m.
A group of green-building experts, coordinated by sponsor Blue Egg, will be on hand to answer questions.

9:00 a.m.	ASHRAE, *Solar Applications for Homes*
10:00 a.m.	Xantrex, *Enabling Solar Energy*
11:00 a.m.	Honeywell, *Creating Differentiation in a Cooled Housing Market*
12:00 p.m.	NAHB, *Introduction to the National Green Building Program*
1:00 p.m.	DOE, *Zero Energy Homes*
2:00 p.m.	USGBC, *LEED for Homes Program*
3:00 p.m.	DOE, *Solar Hot Water System Performance*
4:00 p.m.	BP, *Solar for Builders*
5:00 p.m.	PATH, *Presolarizing: What to Do Before You Innovate*

A Look at the Competition

Just like the well-known Olympic decathlon, the Solar Decathlon consists of 10 contests. But the Solar Decathlon centers on all of the ways in which we use energy in our daily lives — at work, at home, and at play.

To compete, the teams must design and build energy-efficient homes that are powered exclusively by the sun. The homes must be attractive and easy to live in. They must maintain a comfortable temperature, provide attractive and adequate lighting, power household appliances for cooking and cleaning, power home electronics, and provide hot water. These houses must also power an electric vehicle to meet essential transportation needs.

The competition is an exciting time for competitors and spectators alike, but it is not without challenges and conflicts. For example, the public wants to tour the homes, but the juries need unfettered access to the homes to judge each entry fairly and to discuss its merits privately. This means that some of the homes must be closed to visitors during the public tour hours when the various juries are making their rounds. Rest assured that most homes will be open at these times, and Solar Decathlon staff and volunteers can direct you to them. Please note that there are no public tours at all on Wednesday, October 17, when all of the houses must be closed for 24-hour temperature and humidity monitoring.

Scoring

Contests are scored in three ways:

1. By measuring performance (such as meeting temperature and humidity requirements)
2. By completion of contest-related tasks (such as washing laundry or dishes)
3. By the evaluation of juries made up of experts in architecture, engineering, and other appropriate fields.

Some contests are scored subjectively by only the evaluations of the juries, some are scored objectively by only performance and task completion, and some are scored by a combination of these methods.

The Ten Contests

Architecture

Teams are required to design and build attractive, high-performance houses that integrate solar and energy efficiency technologies seamlessly into the design. Architecture is crucial; teams can earn up to 200 points, more points than any other contest. A jury of architects tours the houses to judge this contest.

Engineering

The Solar Decathlon houses are marvels of modern engineering, and this contest "checks under the hood." A jury of engineers evaluates each house's building envelope, indoor environmental control, and mechanical, electrical, and plumbing systems. A jury of energy analysts assesses the teams' use of simulation tools to inform design decisions and predict annual energy performance.

Public Tour Hours	11 a.m. to 3 p.m.	10 a.m. to 5 p.m.	10 a.m. to 5 p.m.	11 a.m. to 3 p.m.
Contests	**Friday, October 12**	**Saturday, October 13**	**Sunday, October 14**	**Monday, October 15**
Architecture (200 points)		Architecture Jury tours team houses		◁)) 10:00 a.m.
Engineering (150 points)				
Market Viability (150 points)		Market Appeal Jury tours team houses		
Communications (100 points)	Opening Ceremony at 10:00 a.m.	Communications Jury tours team houses		
Comfort Zone (100 points)				Temperature and humidity m
Appliances (100 points)				Refrigerator and freezer tem clothes washing and drying
Hot Water (100 points)				Shower tests
Lighting (100 points)				Lighting Jury tours team hou measurements
Energy Balance (100 points)				Measurements of energy in
Getting Around (100 points)				Teams drive for mileage cre

Competition Schedule

By the time the teams arrive on the National Mall, some contest activities have already been completed, but the majority of them occur while the village is open. To accommodate contest activities such as judging and taking measurements, some of the houses will be closed some of the time during public hours.

Market Viability

This contest evaluates whether the house has market appeal and is well suited for everyday living — and if it could be built easily and accommodate a variety of potential homeowners. A key goal of the Solar Decathlon is to help reduce the cost of building-integrated PV systems. Teams build their houses for a target market of their choosing and are asked to demonstrate the potential of their houses to keep costs affordable within that market.

Communications

Each team must produce its own Web site and provide house tours to visitors on the National Mall. Points are based on the success of the team in delivering clear and consistent messages and images that represent the team's vision and results.

Comfort Zone

Teams are scored on their ability to provide interior comfort in their houses by controlling temperature and humidity. Full points are awarded for maintaining narrow temperature and relative humidity ranges inside their houses.

Appliances

The Appliances contest is designed to replicate appliance energy use in the average U.S. home. Points are earned for maintaining a certain temperature in refrigerators and freezers, washing and drying towels, cooking meals and hosting a dinner party for their neighbors, using a dishwasher, and operating a television/video player and a computer during the day.

Hot Water

This contest demonstrates that solar hot water systems can supply all the hot water that households use daily for bathing, laundry, and dishwashing. Teams score points by successfully completing "shower tests" over 5 days of the competition. They aim to deliver 15 gallons of hot water in 10 minutes or less.

Lighting

Points are awarded based on the elegance, quality, and energy efficiency of the lighting design during day and night. A jury of lighting design professionals evaluates the teams' lighting designs, which are required to integrate both electric and natural light, from both a functional and an aesthetic standpoint. Points for maintaining predetermined lighting levels are also factored into the scoring.

Energy Balance

This contest measures and compares the amount of energy going into the batteries from the solar electric system and the amount of electricity being drawn from the batteries to meet the needs of a home. The goal is to finish the competition having produced as much (or more) electrical energy as the house and car required.

Getting Around

Teams use the "extra" energy generated by their solar electric systems to "fuel" their street-legal, commercially available electric vehicles. Points are awarded based on how many miles each team is able to drive.

·11 a.m. to 3 p.m.	Closed to Public	11 a.m. to 3 p.m.	11 a.m. to 3 p.m.	10 a.m. to 5 p.m.	
Tuesday, October 16	Wednesday, October 17	Thursday, October 18	Friday, October 19	Saturday, October 20	Competition Schedule
	Homes Closed to Public All Day	Engineering Jury tours team houses	2:00 p.m.		
		10:00 a.m.			
10:00 a.m.			Awards Ceremony at 2:00 p.m. Overall Winner Announced	Solar Village is Open	
measurements					
perature measurements, computer and TV/video monitor operation, cooking, dishwashing, tasks					
uses; lighting-level	10:00 a.m.	Lighting-level measurements continue			
o and out of battery system					
dit					

 Awards for subjective contests announced

At the top of the Solar Decathlon "Who's Who" list are the students, whose talent, energy, and commitment are second to none. In the following pages, you will hear from the students in their own words. On this page, we would like to recognize the 2007 Solar Decathlon jurors and organizers.

Jurors

We value the contribution of our distinguished jurors, all of whom are leaders in their fields. For biographical and contact information on these individuals, please refer to the Solar Decathlon Web site (www.solardecathlon.org).

Architecture

Gregory Kiss
Kiss + Cathcart, Architects

Susan Maxman
SMP Architects

Grant Simpson
RTKL Associates, Inc.

Alternate juror:
Ken Wilson
Envision Design

Engineering

Kent Peterson
P2S Engineering, Inc.

Bill Rittleman
IBACOS

Miles C. Russell
GreenRay, Inc.

Energy Analysis

Brent Griffith
National Renewable Energy Laboratory

Sue Reilly
Enermodal Engineering, Inc.

Norm Weaver
Fort Collins Utilities

Market Appeal

Bob Burt
Burt Construction Services

Jim Ketter
Tierra Group

Doug Lowe
Artisan Construction, Inc.

Joyce Mason
Pardee Homes

Economic Analysis

Stuart Bernstein
University of Nebraska, Lincoln at Omaha

David Kline
National Renewable Energy Laboratory

Miles C. Russell
GreenRay, Inc.

Web Sites and House Tours

Jaime Van Mourik
GreenShape LLC

Scott Shepherd
D&R International

Alan Wickstrom
BuildingOnline, Inc.

Lighting

Nancy Clanton
Clanton & Associates, Inc.

Naomi Miller
Naomi Miller Lighting Design

Sandra Stashik
Grenald Waldron Associates

The Architecture jurors compare notes on the merits of the New York Institute of Technology entry in the 2005 Solar Decathlon. Credit: Stefano Paltera, NREL/PIX 14604

Organizers

Director
Richard King, *U.S. Department of Energy*

Project Manager
Cécile Warner, *National Renewable Energy Laboratory*

Rules and Regulations Committee
Michael Wassmer, Chair
Mary Anne Dunlap, Sara Farrar-Nagy, Pamela Gray-Hann, Sheila Hayter, Sally Higgins, Wendy Larsen, Ruby Nahan, Robi Robichaud, and Byron Stafford, *National Renewable Energy Laboratory*

Jim Conway and Tom Meyers, *Colorado Code Consulting*

Dan Eberle, *Crowder College*

John Wiles, *Southwest Technology Development Institute*

Communications and Public Affairs

Drew Bittner, Kevin Brosnahan, Wendy Butler Burt, Henry Gentenaar, Anna Martinez-Barnish, and Christopher Powers, *U.S. Department of Energy*

John Horst, *U.S. Department of Energy/Navarro*

Allison Casey, Sue Donaldson, Shauna Fjeld, David Hicks, Susan Moon, Susan Sczepanski, and Jim Snyder, *National Renewable Energy Laboratory*

ABOUT THE TECHNOLOGIES

Some of the concepts and technologies used in the Solar Decathlon houses are tried and true, while others have seldom — or never — been tried. Learn more about these old and new ideas below.

Compact Fluorescent Lamps (CFLs) — These energy-efficient lamps use less electricity to provide lighting levels comparable to conventional (incandescent) lamps. Reduced electricity consumption (less wasted heat) also means that cooling loads are decreased during the summer months, thus reducing the electricity consumed by air conditioners. CFLs work in standard incandescent fixtures.

Electrochromic Windows — This type of window can be darkened or lightened electronically. A small voltage applied to an electrochromic window will cause it to darken; reversing the voltage causes it to lighten. This capability enables the automatic control of the amount of light and heat that passes through the windows, which allows them to be used as energy-saving devices. For example, darkening the windows in summer reduces solar heat gain and still allows visible light to pass through. In wintertime, the windows can be left clear to let in the sunshine that brightens and warms the house.

Insulation — An excellent place to start making a home more energy efficient is with good insulation, keeping out unwanted heat and cold. R-value is a standard rating for heat transfer resistance. The higher the value, the better the insulation. U-value is the opposite, a measure of heat transfer, so the lower values are better. U-values are generally used for rating windows.

Low-Emissivity Windows — Low-emissivity (low-e) coatings for windows, invented and commercialized in the 1980s, have revolutionized window technology. Thin, transparent coatings of silver or tin oxide permit visible light to pass through, but also reflect infrared heat radiation back into the room. This reduces heat loss through the windows in winter. Low-e windows are available for different climate zones and a variety of applications.

Passive Solar Energy and Daylighting — Considerable amounts of solar energy can be captured for desired heating (while avoiding unwanted heating) without active mechanical systems, simply by properly siting and designing a home. South-facing windows, for example, can let in a lot of heat from winter sun, while large overhangs keep out that solar heat in the summer. Similarly, proper window and skylight placement can provide appropriate light for home activities, reducing the amount of electric lighting that is needed. All of the Decathlon homes incorporate these design principles to some extent.

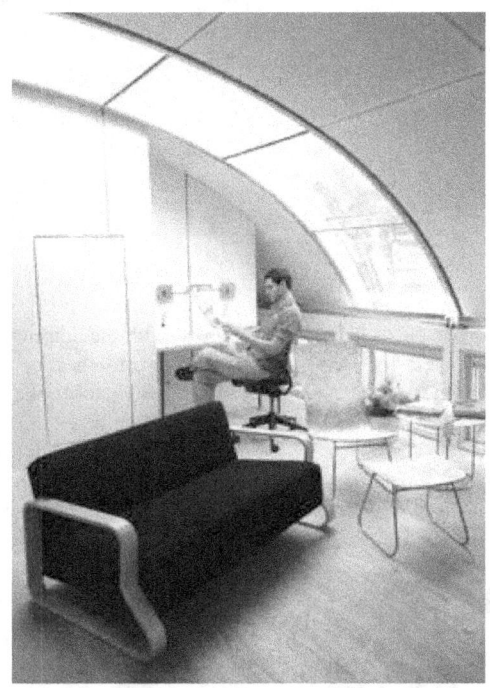

An expansive window follows the roofline of the University of Michigan's 2005 Solar Decathlon house and allows natural daylighting into the work and living spaces. Credit: Chris Gunn, NREL PIX/14268

Phase-Change Materials — It takes energy to change a solid to a liquid or a liquid to a gas (for example, melting ice or boiling water). Conversely, there is energy embodied in the liquid or gas that can be released as heat energy when it liquefies or solidifies. Certain materials with high melting points can store heat (or cold) effectively. In the case of water and space heating in some Decathlon homes, excess hot water or exhaust air is routed through the phase-change material, cooling the water or air and melting the material. When heat is needed, cool water or intake air is run through the phase-change material, absorbing heat from the solidifying material.

PV panels and evacuated-tube solar thermal collectors combine to form an attractive rooftop on Cornell University's 2005 Solar Decathlon house. Credit: Stefano Paltera

Photovoltaics (PV) or Solar Electricity — PV systems are semiconductor devices that generate electricity by absorbing light energy, triggering electrical current flow from an electron-rich material to an electron-deficient one. With building-integrated photovoltaics (BIPV), traditional building components are replaced with PV materials. BIPV materials are used for vertical facades, roofing systems, and shading structures such as awnings. The cost of such a system is offset by the cost of traditional materials that would have been used to finish the building.

Solar Thermal Collectors — Solar thermal collectors use solar energy to heat water or a transfer fluid such as antifreeze flowing through a "collector" designed to capture sunlight. The heated water is then usually stored for use as domestic hot water, but several Decathlon homes also use it for space heating. A couple of the houses are even using the collectors to "fire" absorption chillers for space cooling. Most of the Decathlon homes use better-insulated (but higher cost) evacuated-tube collectors for higher efficiency.

Structural Insulated Panels (SIPs) — These are prefabricated panels typically made of foam insulation sandwiched between sheets of oriented strand board or other building material. SIPs, which are used in many Solar Decathlon houses, offer superior insulation (typically R-4 per inch) and ease of construction.

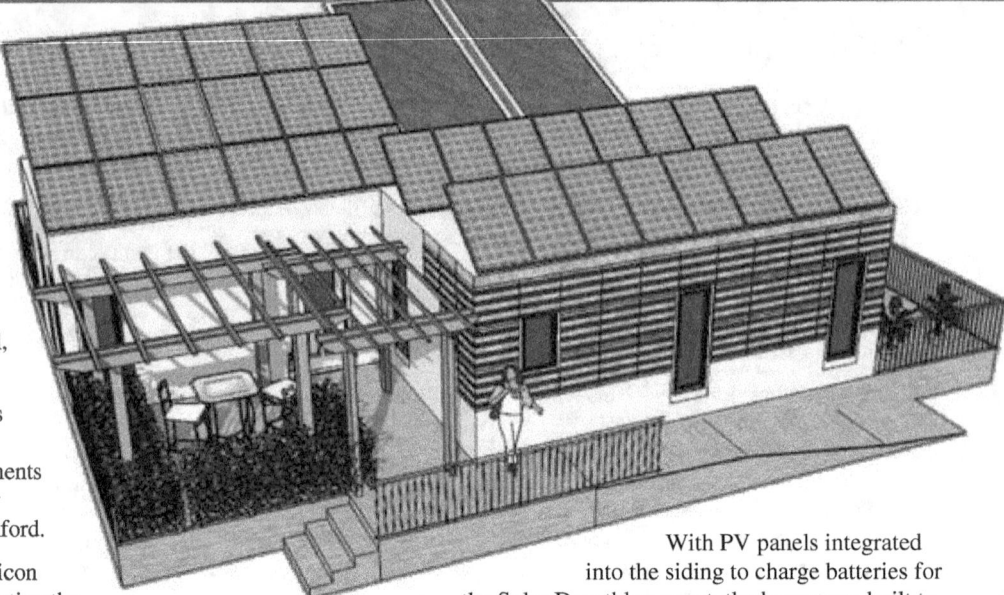

101 SANTA CLARA UNIVERSITY

Purpose Drives Innovation, Gratitude Inspires Giving Back

Design with purpose. This succinct philosophy guided the Santa Clara University team in its quest to build a sustainable solar house that is functional, elegant, intelligent, and innovative.

"Our house is dynamically smart. It uses computers to sense interior and exterior conditions and makes automatic adjustments for thermal comfort and efficient energy usage," says Team Manager James Bickford.

It's not surprising that students from Silicon Valley would take this approach to operating the innovative components incorporated in their house — starting with electrochromic windows. These windows use an innovative glass that, with a flip of a switch, darken to block the sun's rays or lighten to let them in, depending on the temperature desired inside the house.

"Our community has given us enormous support, so we wanted to give back with a very robust outreach effort. This resulted in a heightened awareness of the environment and the importance of sustainability."

— Santa Clara University student Meghan Mooney

Another innovation is a prototype solar thermal unit that can be used for space and water heating as well as air-conditioning. Typically used in large-scale applications such as warehouses, this technology (with absorption chillers) is being used here for the first time in a small space. Santa Clara's house is 727 ft^2 (67.5 m^2).

With PV panels integrated into the siding to charge batteries for the Solar Decathlon event, the house was built to operate off the utility grid. When it returns to campus, it can easily be connected to the grid using an appropriate inverter — and its excess power sold to the utility provider.

Other features that contribute to the house's sustainability are the use of environmentally low-impact materials such as bamboo for I-joist beams, floors, and finishes; energy-efficient appliances; and hybrid lighting using LEDs and compact fluorescents. Glass walls slide open to extend the interior living space onto the deck. South-facing windows and properly sized overhangs allow the sun in during winter and keep it out during the summer.

It's one thing to build a sustainable house; it's another to measure and certify its sustainability. The Santa Clara team uses a unique sustainability meter that quantifies the power used for heating and cooling and measures the amount of carbon emissions the house saves. The collected data could be accessible online, enabling homeowners to adjust their heating and cooling system, appliances, and other devices from a remote location. In the future, this meter could be instrumental in the selling of carbon credits to carbon emitters — motivating Americans to save energy and accumulate carbon credits that can be turned into cash.

Purpose drives these students to innovate, and gratitude inspires them to share their knowledge with the community. "Our community has given us enormous support," says Communication Director Meghan Mooney. "We wanted to give back, so we organized a mini solar decathlon competition among three local high schools." The event resulted in greener schools and a heightened awareness of the environment and the importance of sustainability. ♦

102 UNIVERSIDAD POLITÉCNICA DE MADRID

Designing Casa Solar for American Consumers

The 26-member team from the Universidad Politécnica de Madrid is not the largest one competing in the 2007 Solar Decathlon, but it may be the most diverse. Most of its members are from Spain, but there are also graduate students from Brazil, Chile, Ecuador, Mexico, Peru, Puerto Rico, and Venezuela.

Although the university participated in the Solar Decathlon in the 2005 competition, only one of the students is a veteran. "We built on the lessons learned from the last Solar Decathlon and decided to shift the predominant design concept from Mediterranean to a contemporary design that will appeal to the average American," says Eva Gomez, whose focus is interior design.

"Our objectives are to demonstrate energy-efficient innovation that is applicable to single- and multi-family homes, develop a prototype for commercial manufacturing, and advance the social conscience on sustainability and the environment," says Professor Sergio Vega.

To achieve these goals, they used light construction materials and manufactured-building techniques that allow them to easily customize the house. The house incorporates water-saving technology and solid-state lighting. Electrochromic windows (which darken or lighten to either block or let in the sun's rays), a double envelope, phase-change gels in the foundation, and operable windows help regulate the temperature. A "solar hearth" on the north façade houses PV-charged batteries. The lack of openings on the west eliminates overexposure to the afternoon sun. On the south, the home can be opened directly to an ample outdoor deck that has seating and vegetation.

Inside are lots of colorful doors that screen off rooms such as the kitchen and bath. For convenience, chutes accessible from the kitchen counter allow homeowners to separate refuse into waste and recyclable materials that are fed into outdoor bins situated in a box outdoors on the north side.

This team's social-awareness campaign was impressive. Not only did they get extensive newspaper and television coverage, they transported the first prototype of their house to the SIMA 2007 Property Fair where about 4,000 enthusiastic visitors learned about solar energy and energy efficiency. "Many visitors asked us how they can buy such a house," says Gomez. In addition, when the house was returned to the university, Spain's President, Jose Luis Rodriguez Zapatero, and two ministers were honored guests at an official ceremony coinciding with the España Solar Exhibition.

"Renewable energy is increasingly being supported by the government, with laws being passed to improve construction efficiency and require solar hot water on all buildings," says Benito Lauret, faculty advisor.

Madrid's house is an ongoing project. When it returns to Spain after the Solar Decathlon, the students will continue to refine its systems to improve the technologies further and aim for even greater efficiency.

For the Solar Decathlon, the team members feel confident that they have blended energy-efficient functionality with aesthetics that will appeal to the American consumer, which for them is a very important goal. ♦

"The points of view from so many countries brought out the best in everyone. Brainstorming was very creative and inspired everyone to work harder."

— Universidad Politécnica de Madrid student Maria Perez

103 Universidad de Puerto Rico

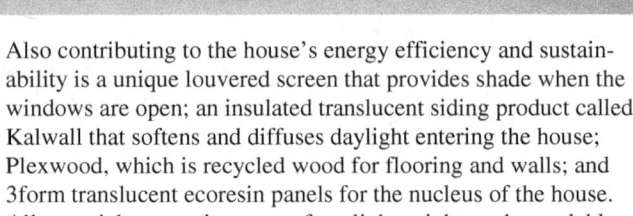

Technology Imitates Life — in this Case, a Single Cell

Biomimicry was the genesis for the Universidad de Puerto Rico's motto: *Technology and Ecology: Partner for the Future*. Biomimicry is a new concept emerging at all levels of innovation. It's the study of nature's best ideas, enabling astute observers to imitate design and process solutions provided by the natural world.

The team took its inspiration from a single cell, which embodies the essence of self-sufficiency and sustainability. The simplest unit of a living organism, the cell produces energy, recycles waste, adapts to changing conditions, functions independently, and communicates with other cells. This is also an apt description of Puerto Rico's solar house: it incorporates everything it needs to be sustainable — it's a living machine.

Sustainability was fundamental to all design and building decisions. "Because we are transporting our house [to the National Mall] by sea and land," says architecture student Fátima Olivieri, "the house is divided and shipped in two pieces." Each piece contains half of the nucleus, or control center. One half incorporates all the electrical equipment including PV modules and batteries, and the other half, the water components such as its solar thermal system.

> *"A valuable experience for me was learning how to work with so many people with diverse educational backgrounds and points of view."*
>
> — Puerto Rico student Marisa Bernal

"We had to look for lightweight materials to construct the house to reduce shipping costs and energy consumption," says engineering student Ferdinand Cardona. "We used Extren fiberglass material for I-beams and columns. It has the same strength as steel, but is so much lighter."

Also contributing to the house's energy efficiency and sustainability is a unique louvered screen that provides shade when the windows are open; an insulated translucent siding product called Kalwall that softens and diffuses daylight entering the house; Plexwood, which is recycled wood for flooring and walls; and 3form translucent ecoresin panels for the nucleus of the house. All materials are maintenance free, lightweight, and recyclable.

Much as the cell adapts to variables in its environment, the Puerto Rico students designed their house to adapt to any environment it might occupy. For instance, the PV panels arranged like a pergola over the roof are tilted 17° to get the most out of solar conditions in Washington, D.C. In Puerto Rico, the angle would be adjusted to 20°, optimizing solar conditions there.

Media attention helped the team members reach out to their audience. The project was written up in two magazines and was covered monthly by local TV news stations. The team members participated in national events such as the Puerto Rico Home Show. During "Solar Week," the team organized a series of activities that included a groundbreaking ceremony and public presentations. Test driving the electric car for the "Getting Around" contest also attracted a lot of attention. "You don't see too many of these cars in Puerto Rico," says Professor of Architecture Jorge F. Ramirez.

According to Ramirez, the project has not only raised the consciousness of the students, but that of the university. "Sustainability is no longer an elective, but a required course in the School of Architecture."

The team feels that the house demonstrates that energy efficiency and sustainability are practical options for comfortable, livable dwellings. "Using the cell as a model for our home put us in touch with the environment and ecosystems and has taught us how to lead cleaner, better lives," concludes Olivieri. ♦

Team Web site: solar.uprm.edu

104 TEXAS A&M UNIVERSITY

Pieces Come Together for a Solar Home

Imagine instead of just moving furniture around when you wanted a change, being able to switch rooms around. The Texas A&M Decathlon team's vision is for a totally modular "plug-and-play" home. "You could swap the position of the kitchen and the bath without a problem, buy an extra kitchen on eBay, or sell off a couple of rooms after the kids move out," says recent architecture graduate Thomas Gerhardt.

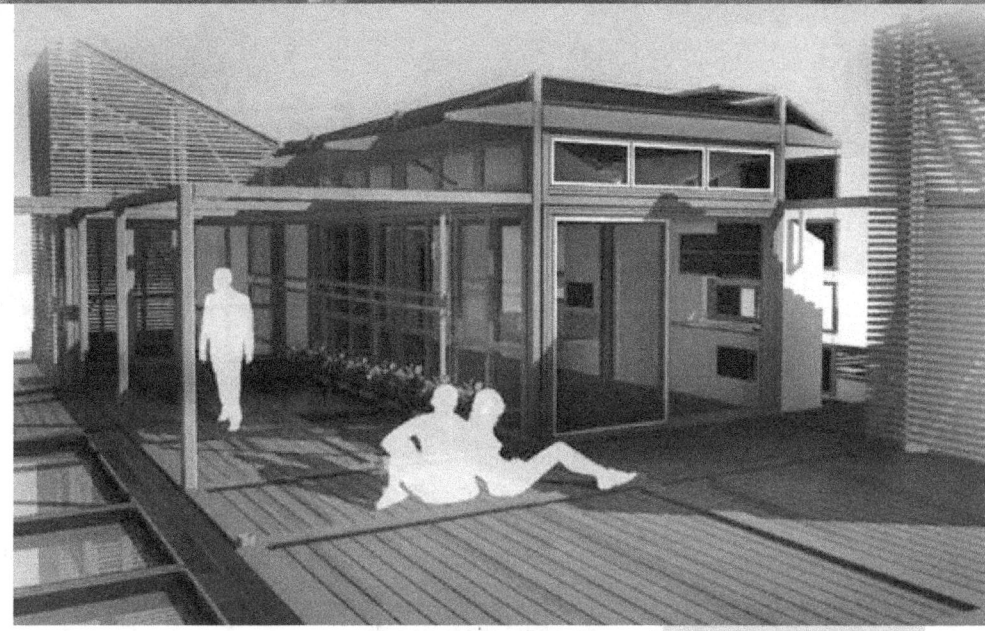

The A&M "groHome" concept is based on interchangeable and interconnected "groWall" units. Some of the 2.5-ft-thick (0.8 m-thick), 10 ft x 10 ft (3 m x 3 m) units will have all of a home's kitchen, bath, or entertainment utilities built into them.

Environmental Design student Josh Canez explains, "All the electricity and plumbing is easy to get to, and the plug-and-play approach will give the homeowner great flexibility, but it made things challenging for us. Everything is interconnected, so whenever we changed one piece, we had to rework everything else to match." This interconnectivity goes both ways: from "groWalls" to the groHome, but also from groHome to envisioned "groCommunities" — whole neighborhoods of coordinated renewable energy homes.

In addition to zero-energy need, a parallel objective for the home is to be suitable for disaster recovery situations. While one version of the home will go to the Mall in Washington, D.C., for the Decathlon, another is being developed to go to Mississippi to replace housing destroyed by Hurricane Katrina. The groHome building system was already being explored on campus when the decision to enter the 2007 Solar Decathlon moved it from the concept stage to reality.

Another distinctive feature of the Texas A&M home is that it is like an animal with two skeletons. An inner skeleton of steel columns and beams provides the basic structure to which a skin of groWall units and structural insulated panels attaches. Then an outer skeleton of cables set 2 ft (0.6 m) to 3 ft (0.9 m) apart from the walls provides support from which the home's PV panels (or other features such as flower trellises) are hung. Just as extra rooms can be easily added, so can extra PV panels to provide power for them. If a hurricane is forecast, the envelope of PV panels can be replaced with "armor."

Hot water for both space heating and domestic water comes from a set of vertical evacuated tube solar collectors on the north side of the house. The lighting plan features CeeLite light-emitting capacitors (as opposed to diodes) that are paper thin, bendable, and can be cut into any shape.

The home also features a major landscaping plan that was designed around the concept of creating a healthy home. It includes a reflecting pool, a wetland that treats the pool water, and even a "bat tower" to provide fertilizer and get rid of insects. The reflecting pool, complete with fish, helps direct light to the solar thermal collectors.

Visitors on the Mall will learn about the home from hand-held PDAs that explain aspects of the home in response to scanning radio-frequency identification tags placed on all the home components and on displays mounted on the deck around the house. ♦

"It has been great to have all this real-world experience in the middle of going to school — pencil sketch to computer model to prototype to actual building. Some of our professors have never been able to do that."

— Texas A&M student Nick Schaider

The BLOOM House

This house is about life and its boundless possibilities; it's also about a budding solar way of life. In fact, the name symbolizes a home that "blooms" like a rose under the sun.

"All the houses use solar. We wanted to take the technology out of the house and make people aware of their surroundings," says Russell Krepart, faculty advisor. For example, wind "blows through the skin of the house." The building's "skin" responds to the wind through shutters that allow for enormous flexibility in terms of light, heat, fresh air, and privacy. Large moveable screens filter light entering from the east and define outdoor spaces.

> *"Our house is called the 'bloom house' because it promotes living your life in bloom. It allows you to live your life to its fullest potential."*
>
> — University of Texas at Austin student Alex Miller

Solar technology is also taken outside. While solar collectors on the roof heat water for the home, the excess heat from the hot water system warms a hot tub outside. "The innovation is using a thing of joy like a hot tub as a technical amenity, as well — it takes heat out of the system so you don't pay for heating the tub," says student Jack Wingerath.

The home's orientation also considers the environment for maximum passive solar performance. Windows are well placed to "pull breezes" from the outside. The south-facing windows also feature louvered screens that block sunlight during the summer, yet allow more warm sunlight inside during the winter when the sun is lower in the sky. The home uses a passive means of lighting as much as possible. Students tried to find a balance between natural light and artificial lighting.

Interior materials are both sustainable and Texas-influenced to create an inviting interior. The floors are mesquite wood, which is native to Texas. The "Texas-sized kitchen" contains state-of-the-art appliances that enhance convenience and energy efficiency. A trivection oven cooks food quickly and thoroughly, while an induction cooktop transfers more heat directly to the food than traditional ranges.

A 7.6-kW PV system, together with a roof brim, form the roof of the house that invites people in with its butterfly shape and proudly displays its technology. Students designed the PV system at a static angle, but it can be customized to the latitude where it will be installed for optimal solar exposure.

"For me, the surprising thing was that the technology is readily available in Austin," says student Matt Brugman. "I didn't have to go far to get things done. I thought this project would be about finding new information, but professionals out there are installing this everyday."

Although the home is high tech, the students used standard materials found in most home improvement stores. "We wanted to take the fear of using the technology out of the system and give people a starting point," says Krepart. "It's technical, but you can do creative things with it."

The struggle is to make the house livable and appeal to the general public and still be efficient, says Krepart. "People don't buy ugly things. The problem we're running into is the Europeans are more advanced as far as energy efficiency. We can get those things here, but we run into a problem with code compliance and such. So what we've tried to do is be conscious design wise. If it's ugly, people aren't interested no matter how energy efficient." ◆

106 UNIVERSITY OF CINCINNATI

A Way with Walls

The main living area of the University of Cincinnati Solar Decathlon project houses the living and dining rooms and kitchen in a single airy space with no dividing walls. Innovative walls, however, are key to the home's inventive design.

The living space is particularly airy because the whole south-facing wall separating it from the home's courtyard is glass. That glass wall also lets in warming sunlight in the winter and provides abundant daylighting. The wall's specially produced triple-pane, low-e glass maintains excellent insulation, and louvered shades keep out unwanted solar heating in summer.

Ingenuity is evident in the rest of the home's walls, as well. All walls have clerestory windows to complete the home's daylighting system. All are also clad with a Formica rain screen separated by 3 in. (7.6 cm) from the main walls to reduce pressure on them — a novel use of a material normally found inside a home.

"Novel, environmentally friendly, and efficient material use was a main goal," says architectural graduate student Christopher Davis. The team sought to have the solar technology drive the design and not look like something attached as an afterthought. The cladding theme of the rain screens is continued in the use of solar electric panels as an integral layer of the entire south-facing roof.

The most distinctive feature of the Cincinnati Decathlon home, however, is a wall that stands separate from the house. A "fence" of 120 evacuated tube solar thermal collectors forms the outer wall of the courtyard. This number of tubes far surpasses any past or present Decathlon entry. In exchange for the donation of the tubes, the team will monitor and share data on their operation with the manufacturer.

Hot water from these collectors is used and reused to cool and heat the home and provide domestic hot water. How can hot water be used to cool a house? This is done via an absorption chiller, which uses energy from the hot water for cooling. Hot water from the solar collector tubes flows into a "hot" storage tank, from which it goes to either the absorption chiller or a heat exchanger for the home's forced-air heating and cooling system, depending on the season. (The same fans used for heating and cooling run at low speed to provide fresh recovery air for the airtight home when no heating or cooling is needed.) The "spent" hot water then flows to a "warm" storage tank to be put to work again. Both the domestic hot water system and a radiant floor heating system draw from this tank.

"The absorption-chilling system is the key technological element that we worked into the home's design," says engineering student Brian Zimmerly. The Spanish-made system is one of only two residential-scale systems that the team could find.

In keeping with the high-tech design, a "digital family" will be on hand to escort visitors through the home. Cartoon plaques of an architect father, businesswoman mother, and engineering whiz kid child posted throughout the home and along the ramp leading up to it will explain its design and how it works. Zimmerly sees the home design as one that "works both inside the box of the competition rules and goes beyond to apply to real-life use." ♦

"The Solar Decathlon experience has been really neat. I am in awe of the amazing things our team has done."
— University of Cincinnati journalism student Jamie Woods

107 UNIVERSITY OF MARYLAND

Branching out in Maryland

When designing their house, University of Maryland students drew inspiration from an unlikely source — the simple, yet vastly complex leaf. "We see the leaf as nature's most efficient organism," says Brittany Williams, student and one of the leaders of the architectural team.

So Maryland's "LEAFHouse" was born. Inside the house, at the ridge of the ceiling, exposed steel supports "branch out" from a wooden spine. This, along with a large expanse of glass, brings light and the feeling of nature into the house. Architecturally speaking, there's a strong connection between the exterior and interior of the house, with a green wall of plants on the south side.

"Just as the leaf changes throughout the year, so can this house, given the mood of the owner," says Jake Zager, student and co-manager of construction. The team sees a need for transformability in today's housing. This transformability takes many forms through both large and small features in their design. For example, the interior features a series of movable, translucent panels that transform a small house into a large space.

Adding to the airy feel is the lighting plan. "We have some enormous south-facing sliding glass doors that admit substantial light and open up views to the outside," says John Kucia, student and co-manager of construction.

> *We've learned how to integrate among disciplines, because we encouraged input from all disciplines from the beginning. We've learned about the great need for communications — from our mentors and from each other."*
>
> — University of Maryland student Brittany Williams

Translucent polycarbonate skylights, filled with nanogel for a higher R value than glass, traverse the length of the house. In coordination with the electrical system, the team is incorporating DMX, a lighting protocol used in theaters that will add a dramatic element to the space. "Think of this as industrial-strength lighting," says Kucia.

The nature motif carries over to the technical side of the design. "The leaf is the ultimate solar collector. We emulate that with the systems in our house," says Nirmal Mehta, student and engineering team leader.

Mehta is particularly proud of the team's smart-house system called SHAC (for Smart House Adaptive Control). Two undergraduate computer engineering majors built a sensor network to bring the comfort level of the home to the ideal. The design network monitors humidity, temperature, light, and whether the doors are open or closed — it's a Web-enabled system that can even factor in weather forecasts. "We're putting the workload on the computer to make better decisions about energy efficiency," says Mehta.

"But we want to make sure 'Hal' isn't running the house," Kucia says. "The humans can always override it."

The most innovative feature of the Maryland house may be the indoor waterfall — a liquid desiccant wall system fully contained behind glass — that evokes the spirit of the Chesapeake Bay area. As far as the team knows, such a system has never been used for a home. A Maryland professor mentored the team and led them through the design process. This experience became a learning process for faculty and students alike.

The team has drawn on other university and community resources as well, with faculty and local industry professionals logging countless volunteer hours. Maryland Decathletes from the 2002 and 2005 competitions mentored this year's team.

"Our support system is strong," says Zager. "We've learned that the true benefit of the competition is the effort we put into it and how much we grow from doing this." ♦

Team Web site: solarteam.org

108 CORNELL UNIVERSITY

Raising the Bar on Sustainability

How do you keep more than 100 students from architecture, engineering, and business disciplines focused on building a futuristic solar house? "Streamlined teams, flexibility, continuous meetings, and consensus building," says Andrew Chessen, who leads the business team. "We're committed to working together in a meaningful way so that all team members have a fundamental understanding of what everyone is doing and how everything is integrated."

Cornell's organizational strategy parallels the unique construction of a "Light Canopy," which is adapted to their solar house. The Light Canopy's streamlined framework of steel trusses serves as a support for PV, evacuated tubes for solar water heating, and a series of vegetated screens that provide shade in the summer.

This framework allows homeowners a great deal of flexibility in how they integrate renewable energy systems because it can also be set up independently of an existing structure. For example, they can add, remove, and rearrange components with relative ease. The structure can also be used to support rainwater collection devices, shelving, lighting, bike racks, and even suspended furniture.

Cornell has a reputation for being particular — the team performed strongly in the 2005 Solar Decathlon and brought home second-place honors. "Cornell didn't need to build another house," says David Bosworth who leads the architecture and construction team. "But we do need to raise public awareness and encourage public adoption of residential solar energy." That's what inspired the students to push the envelope in building a house that is efficient, flexible, affordable, attractive, and adapts to the needs of a changing society.

"It's as if the house anticipates the next technology and is ready for it."

— Cornell student Kristen Distefano

Cornell also takes great pride in the fact that all decisions are made by students. The student-led teams decided to use high-end, although not extremely rare technologies, so that they could more easily demonstrate to consumers how to integrate commercially available renewable energy and energy-efficient devices. "The house is designed to be highly efficient and easy to maintain and upgrade," says Kristen Distefano, who co-chairs the architecture and construction team with Bosworth. The use of raised flooring also allows ductwork and wiring to be easily upgraded.

Honoring their commitment to educate their peers and the public, the team members not only invited green building design and sustainable living experts from industry and academia to educate themselves and other students, they coordinated a variety of educational activities in their local community. They worked with Ithaca city schools to introduce students to solar energy and energy efficiency, collaborated with Cornell's Ecology House on an Earth Day celebration event, and set up demonstrations at the local Ithaca Farmers Market.

"This hands-on experience has no doubt shaped the career directions of many of our students and changed the way they view the environment," says Faculty Advisor Matthew Ulinski.

Bernardo Menezes, engineering team lead, agrees. "The independent nature of the team is what made this experience so valuable. The students decided the direction of the project, and this gave us a sense of ownership."

With a heightened sense of commitment, team members learned about energy-producing and energy-saving components using advanced energy-modeling techniques. They considered properties such as recyclability, pollution potential, production waste, and efficiency of every product they used. But more importantly, they are demonstrating how anyone anywhere can start enjoying a sustainable lifestyle. ◆

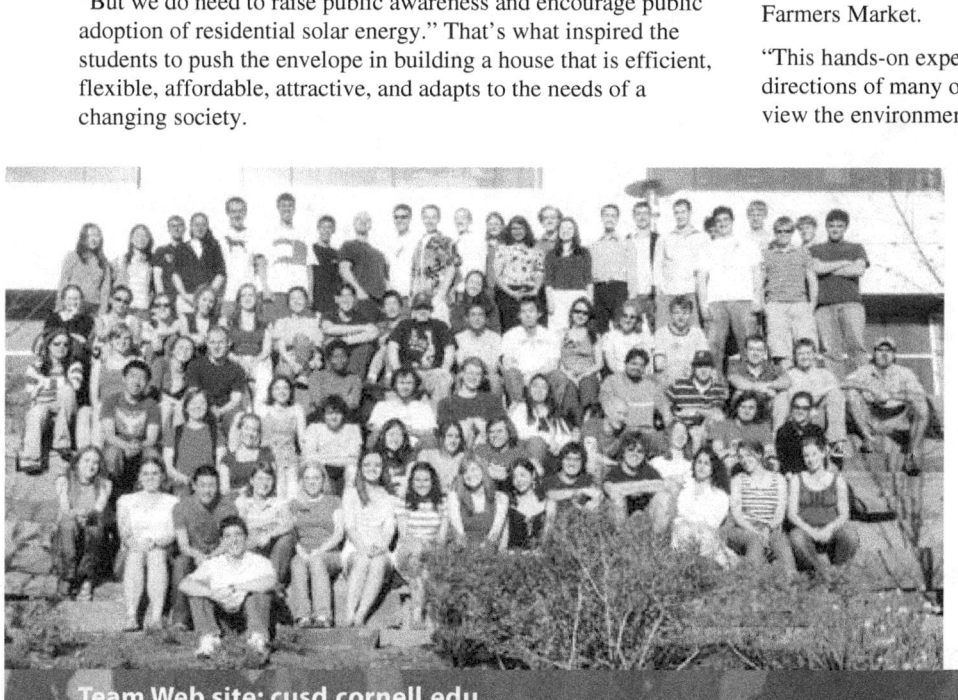

Team Web site: cusd.cornell.edu

Good Things Come in Threes

What happens when your university has entered three Solar Decathlons, producing three distinct solar houses? In the case of the University of Missouri-Rolla, an on-campus solar village happens, replete with student housing and unparalleled research facilities.

"Our overriding goal every year has been to focus on the public and present solar energy in a way that appeals to them," says Jacob Colbert, one of the student team leaders. But the team also seeks to investigate something new each year and establish research opportunities for current and future students and faculty.

They share the view that architecture is important, but their goal as a team is to further solar and renewable energy. "To do that, we are seeking to optimize both energy efficiency and energy production to reach a balance," says Travis Brenneke, student and building project manager. "This is about showcasing not just what solar energy can do or a futuristic design, but striking a balance that will appeal to the masses and not go overboard in either direction."

Automated systems have captured the attention of the 2007 Missouri-Rolla team. Integral to this is a home automation system with indoor and outdoor sensors that will control air-conditioning, lighting, and windows. For example, the system "suggests" when the "energy sensible" thing to do is open the windows rather than turn on air-conditioning. The system can be customized, and the team will use this feature to add a home audio system.

"We wanted our house to be an economical option for people. We believe an average middle class family should be able to afford it."

— University of Missouri-Rolla student Travis Brenneke

The house takes advantage of natural light by incorporating many south-facing windows. A 12-ft (3.7-m) folding glass wall brightens the main living space. In the center of the glass is a door for egress — or the entire wall can be opened so the interior spaces joins up with the deck. This adds a nice touch for the homeowner in terms of appeal and comfortable living, which the team finds worth the energy cost of glass versus a solid wall.

The exterior of the Missouri-Rolla house is finished in Paperstone rain screen, which is UV resistant, easy to install, available in a multitude of colors, and 100% recyclable. Countertops are 50% recycled materials, and the floors are eucalyptus, which is harder and more resilient than bamboo flooring. And the supplier uses good forest-management practices.

At 7 kW, the PV system is much larger than Missouri-Rolla teams used on their 2002 and 2005 entries, which were 5 and 3 kW, respectively. "This year, we want to be able to compete in the 'Getting Around' contest," says Colbert.

A great source of pride for the Missouri Decathletes is that everybody on their team has fingers in all aspects of the project. "We've gotten everybody involved with design, fundraising, building ... everything," says finance student Adam Smith. "This is a real-world experience that makes us more marketable when we graduate."

At home in Rolla, Missouri, the team has extended the welcome mat to their solar village. "We have an open-door policy," says Colbert. "If people drop by or e-mail us, we're more than happy to give a tour. We're very excited to showcase to the public." ♦

110 KANSAS PROJECT SOLAR HOUSE (KANSAS STATE UNIVERSITY AND UNIVERSITY OF KANSAS)

Zero-Energy Technology Rolls across the Prairie

"Go mobile" — one of five points in the Kansas Project Solar House mission statement — gives a good start at characterizing the home the team designed. Transporting the homes to Washington, D.C., is a major challenge for many of the teams, but the virtually fully assembled Kansas entry fits on one truck. A second truck is used to carry solar panels and other additional components.

"It can be unloaded from the truck and set up in a matter of hours," says engineering student Brad Lutz. "On the way back from D.C., we will be stopping at major Kansas cities to display the home." The team is hoping that thousands of Kansans will visit the home and become acquainted with the concept of a net zero-energy home (one that produces as much energy as it consumes during the course of a year).

The home's extensive use of structural insulated panels makes it very "low labor." "We were able to build the home in just eight days," says architecture student Matt Teismann. "It should be ideal for off-grid vacation homes." The home's long, narrow shape is uniquely suited for showing off its renewable energy and energy efficiency features. A façade of solar panels easily attached to standing-seam metal roofing covers most of the south wall, right at eye level and tilted at 64° to maximize winter sun. The panels are integrated as the exterior face of the building.

Three additional panels on the roof are mounted on two-axis tracking systems to maximize energy capture. "We wanted the house to be a true demonstration of solar power at the residential scale," says Lutz.

Another point in the Kansas mission statement is to "redirect expectations," and the home challenges visitors to do just that. It demonstrates that you don't necessarily need heat or artificial lighting for common household tasks. A centrifugal clothes dryer uses a fraction of the energy of a conventional heated dryer. An induction cooktop heats only the cookware and the food inside it, never getting hot to the touch. Backup water heating is at the point of use instead of keeping a storage tank hot. A translucent polycarbonate north window wall and skylights provide daylighting. Indirect fluorescent lights blend with the daylighting, with only a few LED can lights for task lighting. The translucent windows emit a soft glow at night.

"This has given me a career path. I know now I want to be involved in renewable energy or green building. I knew nothing about solar before this."

— Kansas State University student Brad Lutz

The home's sophisticated monitoring and control system, developed by Siemens Building Technologies, directs all utility systems, turning systems off when they are not needed or if the home's energy supply is low. As a backup though, batteries hold three days worth of energy.

The Kansas team members made extensive use of recycled and reclaimed materials. Finishes include reclaimed wood from a deconstructed barn they tore down themselves, recycled-glass Enviroglas terrazzo concrete, and sustainably harvested wood flooring and exterior decking. These building material choices reflect the team's central mission statement point — "to celebrate this place, to be an ambassador to represent the state of Kansas."

Future plans for the home are to use it as a research center, to keep monitoring its operation, and to use it to try out new technologies as they become available. Architecture student Tim Sherman describes the Decathlon as "an amazing learning experience, one of the best so far in my career." ◆

111 UNIVERSITY OF COLORADO AT BOULDER

Thinking Big While Staying Small

When you're the two-time champion of the Solar Decathlon, you have two ways to go: either try to perfect your previous entry to maximize your winning potential or take another approach altogether. Never ones to take the easy route, the team from the University of Colorado at Boulder is striking out in a new direction, with a focus on creating a marketable house.

"We're looking at it from a broader perspective," says Michael Brandemuehl, an associate professor in the Department of Civil, Environmental, and Architectural Engineering. "In some ways, we're really trying to look beyond the competition to production homes in general. We're designing and building a full-size house to make our story more relevant to homeowners as well as the building industry."

> *"The beating heart of our mechanical system is a heat pump with two storage tanks — one hot and one cold — so we can capture energy from the environment when it's available, store it in our tanks, and use it when we need it."*
>
> — University of Colorado graduate student Justin Spencer

Because the Colorado team considers the Solar Decathlon size guidelines too limiting, they've actually designed a much larger house, at 2,100 ft^2 (196 m^2). To make this work in the competition, the 700-ft^2 (65-m^2) central core of the house works as a home in its own right and will be built and brought to the competition in October. Decking around the house will demonstrate the outline of the full house.

"We have designed it as a full house, with just a piece that detaches," says Sara Hrynik, who recently graduated with a degree in environmental design, "and then we have continued to work on all of the details within the competition module to make sure that it is just as pristine and beautiful and interesting as the rest of the house."

The Colorado team is also emphasizing prefabricated housing. The core or "spines" of the house — including the heating and cooling systems, electrical service, laundry, and kitchen — are all enclosed within two modified shipping containers. If the concept were commercialized, the core of home could be assembled in a day by delivering the two containers to the job site, with all the plumbing and electrical lines and major mechanical components pre-installed.

"The coolest thing about our house," says Hyrnik, "is that we have designed the mechanical spines so that they can be shipped and built almost anywhere, allowing the homeowner to build the rest of the house with local materials in the local vernacular. 'Prefabricated' does not mean that everything has to be the same in every house."

Using shipping containers to build prefab housing is a concept drawing quite a bit of attention in architecture circles, in part because of the potential cost savings. In the case of the Colorado team, the concept also fits perfectly with the Solar Decathlon, because it will allow the team to easily ship it across the country.

But for these students, the work is not complete when they return from the Solar Decathlon, because that's when they'll build the remaining 1,400 ft^2 (131 m^2) of the home, including three more bedrooms, two more baths, a breakfast nook, and additional living space. On the plus side, though, that plan is also a major source of funding. The enterprising Colorado students have already sold the final structure to the team's primary sponsor, Xcel Energy, which will use it as a permanent facility for research, education, and outreach to both the industry and the public. ◆

112 TECHNISCHE UNIVERSITÄT DARMSTADT

Germany's Newest Export Product

"Made in Germany" is a phrase that applies well to the Solar Decathlon entry from the Technische Universität Darmstadt. The team members want to present the German way of building, showcasing German technologies and materials in their solar house, including German oak.

The emphasis on "Made in Germany" products and technologies is apparent in the team's collaboration with German companies and manufacturers, such as Bosch, which provided three-month internships in its development department for two Darmstadt students. That arrangement provided a test bed for the students to study the performance of the systems that will provide hot water and climate control for the house.

"It was very interesting because we had all those experts right next to us, and when we had specific questions, we always got very good answers very quickly," says Toby Kern, an architecture student who was one of the interns.

Given Germany's love affair with high technology, you might expect Darmstadt's entry to be a paragon of technology, a finely tuned clockwork mechanism of precision-engineered parts. But you'd be wrong.

"We definitely have high tech in this home," says Kern, "but first we wanted to try to use the low-tech passive way to condition the house and to conserve energy with a highly insulated building shell. When we see that that's not enough, then we also use the high-tech techniques to heat or cool or gain energy and to provide a high comfort level."

But that's not to say that the Darmstadt house isn't filled with its share of technology. Along with highly efficient appliances, the house incorporates phase-change materials in the ceiling and in the north and south walls. Microcapsules of paraffin embedded in the walls change from a solid to a liquid as they are heated, providing an efficient and lightweight means of storing energy within the walls of the home.

The north and south sides of the house are transparent, and oak louvers on all sides provide shading and privacy, but even these louvers incorporate advanced technology. The Darmstadt team has incorporated solar cells into the east, south, and west louvers, so they generate power while providing shading. A tracking system automatically tilts the louvers to follow the sun during the day, maximizing the shading and the production of power from the louvers.

After the Solar Decathlon, the house will return to Germany to be used as a solar power plant, as part of the university's project called the Solar Campus ("Solare Lichtwiese"), through which all buildings on campus will be equipped with building-integrated PV, feeding electricity into the German power grid.

Germany has a "solar feed-in tariff" that provides a guaranteed price for any solar power that is fed into the German power grid. Because the feed-in tariff is high enough to more than cover the cost of the installation over the long term, the university is selling shares to the public to finance these PV systems; this yields a return for the investors as the revenue from selling the power is split among them. The Solar Decathlon house will be the first piece in this ambitious project — continuing to showcase the potential of building-integrated solar power generation. ♦

> *"One of the main criteria for our house is that we actually feel the different seasons and daytimes; that we live in the house, but also experience nature in the house as well."*
> — Toby Kern

113 GEORGIA INSTITUTE OF TECHNOLOGY

Bring on the Sun!

It's a perennial challenge for architects and engineers — how do you open up a building to sunlight without creating glare and overheating the interior space? And how can you maintain a tight, well-insulated space that still has a bright, expansive, mood-enhancing ambience? The team from Georgia Tech is taking on that challenge with gusto. They are bringing on the sun … playing with light to see how it can transform and open up a living space.

"We've placed a great emphasis on light and bringing light into the house in unique ways," says Jason Mabry, a recent Architecture graduate and co-leader of the construction project. "Visitors will be able to see how the house works within itself. They'll see all the technologies we're putting into the house to make it more livable and efficient."

The approach is most obvious in the use of translucent walls, made of two sheets of polycarbonate that enclose an aerogel filler. Aerogel, sometimes referred to as "solid smoke," is the lightest solid known. The material is an excellent insulator and is translucent, allowing filtered light to enter the home. Light is also admitted through a clerestory, a row of clear windows above the walls of the house.

> *"Here we are, with the house almost completed, by students who have little or no professional experience. We have built our house, and that's really significant. It's not a timesheet thing."*
>
> — Georgia Institute of Technology Architecture graduate Joe Jamgochian

Even the building's roof transmits natural daylight. Made of translucent film, the lightweight roof comprises two layers — one of aerogel that insulates and another on top of that to shed water and drain the roof. Architecture student Alstan Jakubiec did the design drawings for the custom-built roof. "It's really exciting to have it on the house — this product is normally used for big installations like football stadiums," he says.

The solar panels are mounted just above the roof and tilt to follow the sun, maximizing power generation while shading the roof from direct sunlight. The roof will generate nearly 6 kW of power, while a vertical solar panel rain screen on the south wall adds another 2.5 kW.

Jason Brown, an engineering student who is now pursuing a Ph.D. in architecture, sees many features of the Georgia Tech house as pushing the envelope. "A model-based control system, a PC, runs according to how the house expects itself to operate. It's programmed to use energy in an optimum way, based on the idea that we have a limited budget of energy," he says.

Joe Jamgochian, a recent Architecture graduate who co-leads the construction project with Mabry, relishes the opportunity to work in close collaboration with university professors, engineering students, and specialists in the construction industry. He is particularly proud of the team's work ethic. "There's been a real commitment by a core group of students and faculty to take individual responsibility for our project as a whole," he says. "They think of the potential issues ahead and address them."

Mabry echoes that notion. "You can sit in a design studio all day long, but the reward is to actually build it … to realize your design, build what you've drawn, and see what it's like in the real world."

Brown has his own ideas about impacting the world. "I'm now thinking about going into teaching," he says. "This experience makes me want to teach in a way that gets people excited. Teach it by doing it. Learn it by doing it. That's the greatest thing about the Solar Decathlon." ♦

Team Web site: solar.gatech.edu

114 CARNEGIE MELLON UNIVERSITY

Plug and Play House

"Plug and play" takes on a whole new meaning at the Carnegie Mellon house: the rooms can be easily upgraded or rearranged to suit the owner. The house was designed around three basic concepts: plug-and-play adaptability of the rooms, the house as an exhibit, and sustainability.

Much like adding a new plug-and-play device to a computer, the house itself can be upgraded with smaller or larger rooms. All the rooms are arranged around the home's central core, which contains all the home's mechanical systems. Connections to mechanical supports are installed in the core, and they are easily accessible and adjustable.

The structure of the house is a steel post and beam system with infill panels that support insulation panels and interior finishes. A "pressure-equalized rain screen" prevents cracks and leaks in the exterior walls. Sustainable materials such as high-efficiency insulation and native white oak from Pennsylvania for the exterior were used as much as possible.

The home's solar energy features include daylighting design that maximizes natural light and reduces the need for electrical lighting; a 6.88-kW solar electric system on the roof; and a solar water heating system above the bathroom. All the rooms, which are referred to as "living pods" by the students, have their own junction boxes so electrical use can be adjusted to unique living situations.

To reinforce the sustainable living message, a "greenscape" composed of plants was added to provide insulation. It literally grows from the land, up the walls, and onto the roof, where the plants keep the home cool in summer.

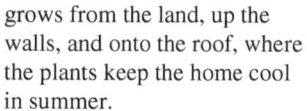

A common space connects the Carnegie Mellon home with the home of the Decathlon team from Germany, softening the edges of the house and reinforcing the sense of community and neighborly interaction.

Inside, energy-efficient appliances and lighting provide more energy savings. Drama students used their stage-lighting experience to create a "lighting mood" in the home and worked with Human Computer Interactions students to create a lighting tool that educates visitors about how and when the home is using electricity.

"We want to encourage the housing industry to use our design system to create homes that families can design around their needs and change them as their needs change, like when they have a new baby or empty nest. It creates a whole new section on eBay!"

— Carnegie Mellon student Ben Saks

"This solar home is a fantastic educational tool for the public and the team," says student Rosemary Lapka. "I can't get the hands-on experience in the classroom I get working on this project. I work with real people, real time tables, and real budgets. It makes it very educational."

Carnegie Mellon worked with two other universities on this project. The Art Institute of Pittsburgh helped students design the furniture. The University of Pittsburgh helped with construction and will install the house permanently after the Decathlon in the Powder Mill Nature Reserve, an outdoor educational center affiliated with the Carnegie Museum of Natural History. At Powder Mill, a "Living Machine" will be added to remove grey water and process it through a series of tanks full of live plants, trees, grasses and algae, goldfish, tiny freshwater shrimp, snails, and a diversity of microorganisms and bacteria to break down waste and turn it into crystal-clear water. ◆

115 PENN STATE

Embracing the Possibilities

When abundant opportunities and possibilities are on the horizon, people often get stuck deciding which ones to pursue. Not so for the Penn State Solar Decathlon team. This high-energy group of students is taking them on one after another.

Take the Market Viability contest, for example, which is new to this year's Decathlon. The Penn State students were inspired by the challenge and ended up building two homes to test their market concept. The competition home, MorningStar Pennsylvania, will serve as a renewable energy research lab and educational residence on campus to inform people about the environmental and economic benefits of sustainable design. Its sister home, MorningStar Montana, will house visiting faculty at Chief Dull Knife College on the Northern Cheyenne Reservation. This affordable version of the MorningStar concept will help advance the use of solar energy in another climate and culture.

"We see our Solar Decathlon home, and the one in Montana, as prototypes where people can learn," says member Sal Gimbert. The team used a hybrid construction process with a mix of prefab and site-built elements. The "Technical Core" of the house (kitchen, bath, mechanical components) is shipped to the home's location, and locally available "materials of opportunity" are used to complete the home.

> *"There is a large breadth of disciplines on our team. It's a big challenge, but a good challenge. You see things in a different light — not just in the way you are trained."*
>
> — Penn State Solar Decathlon Team member Angela Lewis

A big part of their process was to integrate architecture and engineering concepts around energy issues. "We believe this is the key to sustainable design," says Gimbert. This integration appears in many of the decisions made by the Penn State team.

An "Energy Dashboard" will monitor and display energy consumption and production to teach the inhabitants about how they are "spending" their energy. A curtain wall system with PV-powered LED lighting will glow different colors depending on weather forecasts. Pennsylvania bluestone and reclaimed slate shingles will provide thermal mass. And just to be ready for anything, the home's mechanical system includes four ways to heat water.

When a 100-year-old elm tree fell on the Penn State campus, another material of opportunity emerged, and the lumber was put to good use for a student-crafted dining table. Another fallen tree, this one a white oak, became a set of movable sun shades on the south wall. In the living space, the "Movable Wall" can either expand the bedroom or the living and dining area, depending on the needs and moods of the occupants.

The students saw the talent and expertise available at Penn State as yet another opportunity. "From the beginning, we wanted to engage as many university programs as possible. So, we kept the design process open to a range of disciplines throughout the university. Close to 900 Penn State students have been involved in the Solar Decathlon," says member Andreas Phelps.

What's their attitude going into the competition? "We're going for broke," says member Gretchen Miller. "We want to be outstanding representatives for the Penn State community by using the Solar Decathlon as a catalyst to reach our long-term goals. There's no stopping us." ♦

Team Web site: solar.psu.edu

116 MASSACHUSETTS INSTITUTE OF TECHNOLOGY

Learning from the Past

Mens et manus — mind and hand. Staff researcher Kurt Keville cites the historic university motto as the guiding philosophy for the MIT Solar Decathlon team effort. "It is like an intense clinic on architectural terminology. We get to take the analysis and learning we do in class and turn it into the real world — all the way down to insurance and locating the house on the lot so that it would be easier to load on the truck."

Analysis is part of the MIT culture, and the Decathlon team applied it to lessons from the past to craft its vision of housing for the future. An architecture class reviewed and analyzed all the 2002 and 2005 Solar Decathlon entries. Determining that the 2002 Solar Decathlon heat wave is more likely to occur than the 2005 rainstorms, the team designed with the assumption of at least one sunny day for the week. In this spirit, the team sought to minimize conversion losses wherever possible — employing efficient solar cells, a small battery footprint, complete waste mitigation, and maximized solar thermal collection.

Although this is MIT's first Decathlon entry, it is by no means the school's first solar home. The team refers to the home as "Solar 7," because MIT has built six solar homes in the past, going back to the 1930s. Studying the history of these homes helped inspire the new home's primary technological feature, which is an innovative use of solar thermal systems. Passive solar thermal energy storage was a key feature in one of the historic homes. The new MIT Decathlon entry features a Trombe wall of translucent tiles that are used to passively convert sunlight into stored heat.

The home also has two sets of 30 evacuated-tube solar thermal collectors, which heat water flowing to a water storage tank. The tank serves both in-floor radiant heating and domestic hot water, which also includes a backup electrical heater. The team designed the home with lots of cross ventilation and commercial through-the-wall air conditioners for cooling. A flexible system of doors allows the bedroom, office, and great room to be joined or separated, providing a flexible living space. Similarly, a sliding door between the great room and deck lets in breezes to cool the interior while blending the exterior space into the great room.

Separate alternating- and direct-current circuits efficiently use the energy from the home's solar cells. These high-efficiency SunPower PV modules provide the flexibility of more than 8 kW of power. Extensive innovative use of recycled materials demonstrates the effectiveness of sustainable design. These materials include yellow pine beams refurbished from a mill and windowpanes from the John Hancock Building in Boston (which became infamous for popping out of the building) that form a clerestory skylight to daylight the great room.

If you don't make it to the MIT home, you can still tour the home on the virtual reality Web site secondlife.com. Another high-tech feature to help explain the home to visitors will be a touchscreen computer coffee table that interfaces with software controls for the home's utility systems. A comment from a contractor helping the MIT Decathlon team members build their home conveys the spirit of the team: "I've wanted to build a home like this since I was a child; this is fabulous." ♦

> *"The Decathlon experience has been a powerful opportunity to engineer, design, build, and finance the creation of an energy-efficient home."*
>
> — MIT graduate student Corey Fucetola

117 TEAM MONTRÉAL (ÉCOLE DE TECHNOLOGIE SUPÉRIORE, UNIVERSITÉ DE MONTRÉAL, MCGILL UNIVERSITY)

Polar Revolution

You may have heard of the popular new book "Solar Revolution." In a similar vein, Team Montreal students are starting a polar revolution to make solar energy popular in cold northern climates. Their biggest challenge is convincing their northern audience that solar technology can indeed work well in very cold climates.

"We think we've done that," says Joanna Rosvalt, an architecture student from McGill University. "The most important thing for us was to focus on the building envelope. It had to be both functional and aesthetic."

Team Montreal's home starts with a special structural steel frame that is easy to assemble and disassemble, allowing the students to put together the house very quickly. Unlike many teams that use modular homes, the walls (and some of the furniture) are "clipped" directly to the steel frame. Inside the frame, polyurethane insulation made from soybeans and recycled plastic keeps the occupants warm during those cold northern winters. Windows are triple glazed, low-e, and have automated shading, trapping the sun's heat once inside. A green roof and a green wall reduce energy used for cooling and add insulation as well as rain water recovery.

> *"I always dreamed of living in a smart home that could be autonomous and ecological. Isn't it amazing to be able to build one?"*
>
> — Michael Chapman, team president and student at École de Technologie Supérieure

On the roof, 40 PV panels producing 8.2 kW will also be clipped to the structure, so they won't need any other roofing under the PV system, reducing the cost and use of unnecessary materials. In the middle of the roof, two solar thermal collectors heat water for both the radiant floor and household use.

The team tried to incorporate as many locally made and raw materials as possible to reduce the environmental impact caused by shipping. For example, most of the furniture will be made of reused materials.

A unique feature is the use of artificial intelligence for temperature control and energy use. The "house" will search the Web for the weather forecast to predict the amount of energy it will be able to produce in the days to come and how much it will need for its occupants. The system will recommend energy use choices to meet upcoming demands. The system controls heating, cooling, lighting, shading, and ventilation, all with one interface. Unlike traditional energy management systems, this one can get information from several systems communicating with different protocols, so decisions can be made based on more information.

The interface in the house manages the "fueling" of the electric car for the Getting Around contest. The home's interface will say: "The battery is low. Where do you want to consume the energy left tonight? In the car or for the home, and in what proportion?"

How a home is insulated and designed is very important, but so are utility prices, says student Catherine Seers. "Quebec has the cheapest electricity rates in North America. They average about 6 to 7 cents per kWh. PV is too expensive for many Canadians, but solar thermal collectors are cost effective and they work well in winter too. We'll promote solar thermal and energy efficiency products a lot in Canada, because we're showing great savings with those technologies."

Team Montreal is composed of about 40 students who have joined together from three of Montreal's esteemed universities: École de Technologie Supérieure and the architectural schools at the Université de Montréal and McGill University. The team proudly represents Montreal and Canada. ♦

Team Web site: solarmontreal.ca

118 UNIVERSITY OF ILLINOIS AT URBANA-CHAMPAIGN

Assembly Line to Success

What is a Solar Decathlon team to do when the unpredictable Midwest climate interferes with building the house outdoors? If you're the University of Illinois team, you simply build it inside a warehouse.

"We set up an assembly line, a rail system, to construct the home in three modules — we can roll modules out of the warehouse and onto the truck," says student Bob Kinsey. "We have demonstrated our ability to mass-produce these modules in a large-scale environment."

The concept of modular design is not something new, but people may think of it as low quality.

"This is not true for us," says architecture student Nora Wang. "We designed the building to be flexible, comfortable, and livable. And you can customize the interior space, which helps engage the user's imagination."

The students also built energy simulation into their design. "Our model is able to predict how much energy the building will use and how much will be generated by our PV panels," says student Luis Martinez. "Several iterations of our design process used the energy model. This allowed us to study and optimize many of the design parameters, such as insulation thickness."

When it comes to making the house comfortable and easy to live in, the team has this covered, too. "This area may be the most innovative element for us," says student Ben Barnes. Cooling and heating is all radiant via ceiling panels — no forced air is used. Regarding dehumidification, the team is exploring a design that integrates aesthetics and functionality. With delight, Barnes admits to "breaking and rebuilding almost all of the appliances, such as putting in much more efficient compressors to save energy."

The team's approach to lighting also was carefully conceived. Placement of windows and doors for daylighting was designed in parallel with the artificial lighting plan. They are using dimmable fluorescent lights and LED bulbs for task lighting. The students even designed their own reflectors to reflect light onto the ceiling. "The LED was invented by a graduate and current professor at the University of Illinois, so we take great pride in using this technology," says student Susan McKenna.

Every piece of furniture and cabinetry in the home is student-designed and customized with inhabitants' activities in mind. The team used eco-friendly material, such as bamboo and reusable 3form panels. A local firm, which is headed by an Illinois alumnus, built the kitchen cabinets from 100% recycled particleboard. "Our industry contacts are excited to get their products out there. One of the greatest things is the way people have stepped up to the plate," says Wang.

This highlights the team's success with in-kind donations, which became a main component of their funding strategy. For example, the team received four compressors from a Danish company and two from a Brazilian company, both of which are affiliated with the Air Conditioning and Refrigeration Center at the university. "We go to a company and say, 'This is where we see your role in the house of the future.' They see a new market and get excited," says Barnes.

The team members feel certain that the modularity and flexibility of their design translates well to the consumer. "This is about the affordability of a solar home for everyone. It's the Volkswagen of homes," says Kinsey. ♦

> " We have developed a marketable prototype. This 'new solar' house is not just about adding PV panels, it can be a fancy-looking building and comfortable, too."
>
> — University of Illinois student Nora Wang

LAWRENCE
TECHNOLOGICAL
UNIVERSITY

A New Contender

For some teams coming to the Solar Decathlon for the first time, the challenges of designing a home, raising funds, procuring equipment, and actually building the home and bringing it to the National Mall are enough to deal with. Not so for Michigan's Lawrence Technological University, which is aiming to achieve far more than the competition's requirements.

"All of the design choices that we're making and all of the technical choices that we're making are really taking into consideration not only what's good for the competition, but what's good for the environment," says Christina Span, an architecture student.

That includes drawing on locally sourced, sustainable materials, such as decking material made of a composite of rice hulls and polymer. It also means packing the small house chock-full of technology.

One example is the use of structural insulated panels for the walls and ceilings. These prefabricated building components sandwich an insulating foam between two sheets of oriented strand board, creating a highly insulating wall that can be quickly assembled, making construction of the walls and roof a breeze. In addition, electrochromic windows, which can be turned from clear to tinted electronically, control the amount of sunlight coming into the home.

To help cool the house, a "solar chimney" uses the natural tendency of

> *"This competition has just been huge for our university; it has transformed the face of it in some ways."*
>
> — Lawrence Tech student Elliott Schmitt

hot air to rise as a means to channel hot air out of the house. For heat and hot water, the home draws on evacuated tube collectors to produce hot water, which runs through tubes in the flooring to create a radiant heating system.

Achieving an environmentally sensitive design with green materials, innovative efficient products, and a range of solar technologies required the close collaboration of engineering and architecture students, most of whom had never worked together before. The project also raised awareness of green building among many of the team members.

"I realized that green building is going to be an integral part of any engineering project from here into the future," says Chris McCarthy, an electrical engineering student. "I want to increase my knowledge of other systems, and the Solar Decathlon was a great way to start that, and to start me on my way."

Lawrence Tech's cross-disciplinary team has also generated four senior projects for undergraduates, as well as one graduate project. For the architecture students, nearly all are now considering graduate schools with design/build programs, because they realize the benefits of seeing a project through to its final construction.

"That's across the board, as far as the architecture students that have gotten involved," says Christina Span.

The project also has the strong backing of the school, and most important, of the school's alumni. A special campaign sparked the interest of the school's alumni and yielded significant funding for the team.

"We had one of the largest alumni-giving campaigns ever," says Assistant Professor Philip Plowright, who teaches in the College of Architecture and Design. "We've had people give to the university who have never given anything before, because they heard we were doing this." ◆

Team Web site: solar.ltu.edu

120 New York Institute of Technology

Open Minds, Open House

Close your eyes and imagine this house on a beach. The entire south wall, a key feature of the home, opens to the beach, breezes, and natural light.

Students from the New York Institute of Technology named their dwelling "Open House" for two reasons. First, they are targeting beachfront homeowners to show them how solar energy and sustainable design can complement shoreline properties. The students also point out that their design would work well on any property with a good southern view. Second, the term "open house" is an expression of the team's ideal home: a home with influence extending beyond its physical walls… a home that is one with its community and nature.

Integration with nature and the community begins with the architecture. A unique southern wall opens completely to the beach, blending the line between sand and walls. A white ceiling helps to maximize natural light. A contained pond on the roof reflects light back into the open space, which further maximizes daylight and reduces the need for electrical lighting.

The home is filled with low-energy-consuming appliances and lighting. All the mechanical systems are integrated together, making them more efficient. The floors and roof are made from structural insulated panels, a prefabricated product that offers superior insulation and ease of construction.

On the roof, an evacuated-tube solar thermal system collects solar energy for water heating and space heating. A geothermal heat pump uses the roof pond (rather than the more typical underground installation, which can't be used on the Mall) as a heat source to provide extra heating. A building-integrated 7.7-kW PV system doubles as the shading overhang for the south wall.

Despite the home's advanced solar technology, the team was surprised at how tough it is to sell solar to the public. "We didn't realize how much more still needs to be done to have the public embrace solar," says student Daniel Rapka. "People don't realize a solar home operates like a normal home. You don't have to give up anything to live in this home. You can design it around a normal standard of living. You can have a stereo, TV, etc. You can give users everything they want to be happy in their home."

Another layer of integration is the home-automation system or "smart house" feature. This system allows people to get real-time data on energy use. The home-automation system serves as an educational tool by giving the public a user-friendly way to view a home's energy use.

"The smart house feature ties into our open house idea where not only homeowners learn about the house, but homeowners could put their energy-use information up on a blog so the community could share in the information," says student Matt Mathosian. "People could log on to a Web site where they could comment about energy use."

In the meantime, the team plans to educate visitors to the Decathlon with an advanced 3-D tour using handheld computers that take visitors on a tour of the home. Tour elements are also integrated into the house. Educating the community will continue after the event. The team plans to bring the home back to campus and start a new sustainable design center for students. The home will also be used as a guest house for visiting dignitaries. ♦

> *"What inspires us is the notion of a house being part of a community … a house that shares resources with the community … a community where like-minded people share ideas and energy sources."*
>
> — New York Institute of Technology student Matt Mathosian

U.S. DEPARTMENT OF ENERGY
ENERGY EFFICIENCY AND RENEWABLE ENERGY

The mission of the U.S. Department of Energy (DOE) Office of Energy Efficiency and Renewable Energy (EERE) is to strengthen America's energy security, environmental quality, and economic vitality in public-private partnerships that promote technological innovation for buildings, homes, transportation, power systems, and industry.

The need for energy efficiency and renewable energy has never been greater. President George W. Bush has declared that "America is addicted to oil," and he

This house, built by McStain Enterprises under the DOE Building America program, contains value-engineered floors, better insulation, tighter ducts, low-emissivity windows, and controlled ventilation to improve indoor air quality. It also features a solar space-heating and water-heating system. Credit: Nancy Wells, NREL/PIX 13551

called for a new Advanced Energy Initiative to respond to this critical situation. EERE plays an important role in the President's initiative by bringing about commercialization opportunities for new technologies and enabling commercial frameworks to accelerate the development and deployment of clean energy technologies and practices.

Working with industry, state and local governments, and academia, and supported by its National Renewable Energy Laboratory in Golden, Colorado, EERE consists of ten research, development, and deployment programs. These programs are in two distinct branches of research and development — both of which are represented in the office's name.

The first branch includes renewable energy sources: solar, hydrogen, wind, biomass, and geothermal. Developing America's abundant renewable energy resources will decrease our dependence on foreign fuel and strengthen our national security. Renewable energy technologies also produce fewer greenhouse gas emissions and have less impact on the environment. The Solar Decathlon itself is testament to DOE's ongoing efforts to make solar power a larger part of America's energy portfolio.

The second branch of EERE includes technologies that make buildings, transportation, and appliances more energy efficient, and make power transmission more reliable. Many examples of these technologies are on display here at the Solar Decathlon and are incorporated into the homes constructed by the student teams. By using less energy, American families save on their utility bills without sacrificing comfort.

The work of EERE also includes weatherizing the homes of American families in need, supplementing state energy programs, and promoting energy efficiency in federal government facilities and installations.

The DOE mission lies at the cutting edge of science and social responsibility. By creating beneficial energy technologies and making use of "free" energy sources such as the sun, wind, and the Earth's own warmth, we can provide less expensive, more reliable, and more abundant energy for every family in the United States. This is making a difference in the everyday lives of Americans by enhancing their energy choices and their quality of life.

Welcome to the Solar Decathlon and please join us in wishing good luck to all the competing teams. Tour the homes, enjoy your visit, ask questions... and think energy! ♦

Premier Gardens, a highly energy-efficient community in Sacramento, California, generates more than 50% of its own electricity using GE Brilliance Roof Integrated Solar Electric Systems. Credit: GE

NATIONAL RENEWABLE ENERGY LABORATORY

The U.S. Department of Energy National Renewable Energy Laboratory (NREL) is pleased to be a sponsor of the 2007 Solar Decathlon. We welcome competitors from around the United States and the world who have come to compete in this unique and important competition. Sponsorship of the Solar Decathlon is a natural fit for NREL, America's primary laboratory for renewable energy and energy efficiency research and development.

Our laboratory in Golden, Colorado, is home to the National Center for Photovoltaics, where world-class scientists and engineers explore new methods and materials for turning sunlight into electricity. Many of those researchers work in the Science and Technology Facility, which this year was designated one of the most energy-efficient and environmentally friendly places to work in the United States by the U.S. Green Buildings Council under its Leadership in Energy and Environmental Design (LEED) Green Building program. The building is the only U.S. federal facility to earn a LEED platinum rating, which is the highest rating awarded.

Researchers in the NREL Center for Buildings and Thermal Systems also work in laboratory facilities that showcase passive solar design and energy efficiency features. The Thermal Test Facility, which uses only 40% of the energy of a conventionally built laboratory, serves as a test bed for high-efficiency lighting, space conditioning, water heating, and daylighting.

NREL works to nurture a wide range of technologies that benefit America's economy, national security, and environment. Our research portfolio extends beyond solar and building design into wind power, biomass power, biofuels, geothermal energy, hydrogen, fuel cells, distributed power, advanced vehicle design, and basic energy science.

The laboratory celebrated its 30th anniversary in July 2007. In those 30 years, we have successfully developed materials and technologies that have been instrumental in reducing the cost of solar electricity by more than 80%. In the buildings arena, NREL has developed software that helps architects design cost-effective, energy-efficient structures and technologies such as "smart" windows that darken in bright sunlight to help keep buildings cool and comfortable.

By combining energy efficiency with renewable energy technologies, we are working with the nation's homebuilders to advance the concept of "net zero energy buildings"—

structures that produce as much energy as they use on an annual basis.

NREL is an exciting place to work, with researchers exploring the cutting edge of energy science and engineering to meet one of the greatest challenges of our time — developing clean, affordable, secure sources of energy. Solar Decathletes will likewise help the nation shape its energy and architectural future. We at NREL join with our fellow Solar Decathlon sponsors in wishing these student teams continued success throughout the competition and in meeting the challenges that await them.

NREL is a U.S. Department of Energy laboratory managed by Midwest Research Institute of Kansas City, Missouri, and Battelle of Columbus, Ohio. ♦

Secretary of Energy Samuel W. Bodman met several NREL summer interns at NREL's Habitat for Humanity house in Wheat Ridge, Colorado. These interns and dozens of NREL employees constructed the nation's first net zero energy home built for the Habitat for Humanity program. Credit: Jack Dempsey, NREL/PIX 14021

NREL researchers use hot-wire chemical vapor deposition to produce high-efficiency PV devices. Credit: Richard Matson, PIX14602.

The Science and Technology Facility at NREL, pictured below to the right of the Solar Energy Research Facility, was completed in 2006. The facility was designed to help accelerate the development and commercialization of promising new solar energy technologies. Credit: Patrick Corkery, NREL/PIX14765

THE AMERICAN INSTITUTE OF ARCHITECTS

The American Institute of Architects (AIA), a proud sponsor of the Solar Decathlon since its inception, is honored to support academic teams representing universities from around the world as they design and build innovative applications of solar power.

Creative problem solving is something the AIA and its 80,000 members know very well. For 150 years, AIA members have worked with each other and their communities to create more valuable, healthy, secure, and sustainable buildings and cityscapes.

The AIA seeks to dramatically increase the number of high-performance buildings constructed in the coming decades. Buildings account for an estimated 48% of all greenhouse emissions—compared to 27% for transportation. Seventy-six percent of all electricity generated by power plants goes toward operating buildings.

We believe architects are uniquely positioned to have a profound impact on energy usage. The AIA has adopted a position statement calling for the immediate energy reduction of all new and renovated buildings to one-half the national average for that building type, with increased reductions of 10% every five years. By 2035, it is our goal that all buildings designed will be carbon neutral, meaning they will use no fossil fuel energy.

Through our partnership with the U.S. Department of Energy and its Solar Decathlon program, we seek to demonstrate not just the critical connection between building design and energy conservation, but also to take one hopeful step in ensuring a lasting legacy for future generations. ◆

The AIA/COTE (Committee on the Environment) Green Projects Awards recognize projects that address environmental challenges with designs that integrate architecture, technology, and natural systems. Some recipients of the 2007 honors are shown here.

Sidwell Friends Middle School, Washington, D.C.

A pre-kindergarten through 12th grade school incorporates high-efficiency lighting, solar ventilation chimneys, and a PV array that generates 5% of the building's energy needs. Credit: Barry Halkin

Hawaii Gateway Energy Center, Kailua-Kona, Hawaii

This visitor complex is designed as a thermal chimney, capturing heat and creating air movement using only building form and thermodynamic principles. A PV system provides all of the energy needed to run seawater pumps, lights, and other electrical equipment. Credit: Franzen Photography

Z6 House, Santa Monica, California

This single-family residence has no forced-air heating or cooling. The home has a passive cooling strategy that uses cross-ventilation and a thermal chimney. A 2.4-kW PV array is designed to provide up to 75% of the home's energy needs. Credit: CJ Berg Photographics/Sunshine Divis Photography

Global Ecology Research Center, Stanford, California

This building at Stanford University is an extremely low-energy laboratory and office building for the Carnegie Institution of Washington. Proper orientation, exceptional daylighting, sunshading, and natural ventilation set the stage for innovative mechanical systems. Credit: Peter Aaron/Esto Photographics

THE AMERICAN SOCIETY OF HEATING, REFRIGERATING AND AIR-CONDITIONING ENGINEERS

The American Society of Heating, Refrigerating and Air-Conditioning Engineers (ASHRAE) is proud to be a sponsor of the 2007 Solar Decathlon. ASHRAE isn't just about "black boxes" that heat and cool facilities or provide refrigeration. ASHRAE is at the forefront of improving the technologies that make energy-efficient, healthy, and comfortable buildings possible.

The principles and guidance for proper indoor air quality, energy efficiency, and comfort that Solar Decathlon participants integrate into their design efforts are from ASHRAE. The ability to provide a successful alternative-based living environment requires an understanding and proper application of ASHRAE fundamentals covering heating, ventilating, air-conditioning, and refrigerating.

ASHRAE's involvement in the Solar Decathlon is a natural progression from the society's long-standing role in energy guidance. Since being developed in response to the energy crisis in the 1970s, ASHRAE's Standard 90.1, *Energy Standard for Buildings Except Low-Rise Residential Buildings*, has influenced building designs worldwide. The standard has been established by the U.S. Department of Energy (DOE) as the minimum commercial building reference standard for state building energy codes under the Federal Energy Policy Act.

Standards are just one resource provided by ASHRAE to architects and engineers involved in sustainable design. We also provide guidance through our handbook series, educational programs, research program, and special publications.

But ASHRAE is dedicated to providing more than just minimum energy standards. We are working with DOE, the American Institute of Architects, the Illuminating Engineering Society of North America (IESNA), and the U.S. Green Building Council (USGBC) to publish a new Advanced Energy Design Guide series. The series provides a simple approach for contractors and designers to create advanced energy savings.

ASHRAE is also working with USGBC and IESNA to write the nation's first standard on sustainable building design. Standard 189P, *Standard for the Design of High-Performance Green Buildings Except Low-Rise Residential Buildings*, will become the benchmark for all sustainable green buildings in the United States because it is being developed for inclusion into building codes. The real impact of Standard 189P is that ASHRAE, along with IESNA and USGBC, are taking advanced energy conservation guidance mainstream for the general public's benefit.

ASHRAE's 50,000 members around the world are committed to economic energy-efficiency standards and advanced energy-efficiency guidance. We are the foundation of energy conservation in buildings. ♦

ASHRAE is renovating its headquarters in Atlanta, Georgia, as a sustainable building.

Former ASHRAE President Terry Townsend (on the left) served as a judge in the 2005 Solar Decathlon.

ASHRAE provides technical and career guidance to about 5,200 student members worldwide. An extensive student program is held at the society's winter meetings.

The National Association of Home Builders (NAHB) is an enthusiastic supporter of the innovative, environmentally friendly ideals and building technologies promoted through the Solar Decathlon. We are also pleased to sponsor a special award — separate from the competition itself.

NAHB has promoted energy-efficient building techniques for years. When energy prices soared in the late 1970s, we were the first organization to step forward and introduce voluntary energy guidelines for new residential construction. Over the next decade, the energy efficiency of new housing about doubled.

In January 2005, NAHB introduced its voluntary Model Green Home Building Guidelines to the public. In 2006, NAHB took those efforts a step further by starting development on the ANSI National Green Building Standard. This is a collaborative effort of NAHB and the International Code Council. Like the guidelines, the National Green Building Standard (NGBS) is designed to help mainstream builders incorporate environmental practices into every phase of the home-building process while still placing a premium on affordability. The green building practices contained in the NGBS include many of the building techniques you'll see in the Solar Decathlon houses on the National Mall. The NGBS is scheduled for publication in early 2008. NAHB is also in the final stages of developing the National Green Building Program, which aims to further advance mainstreaming voluntary green practices into the housing industry. This program will help communities and builders provide the infrastructure needed to implement the cost-effective NGBS practices community wide.

Although energy efficiency is a key component of the NGBS, we also emphasize careful lot planning and site design, using building resources effectively, conserving water, promoting healthy indoor air quality, and educating new homeowners on how to best use the green features of their new homes.

Our members — all 235,000 of them — will construct about 80% of the more than 1.45 million homes projected to be built in the United States this year. NAHB is committed to advancing energy-efficient building techniques and is excited about our involvement in the 2007 Solar Decathlon. ♦

The National Association of Home Builders (NAHB) and the DOE Energy Efficiency and Renewable Energy Office awarded Team Canada a first-place plaque for building the most energy-efficient house at the 2005 Solar Decathlon. Credit: Stefano Paltera

Built by Stitt Energy Systems of Rogers, Arkansas, winner of 15 EnergyValue Housing Awards, this home demonstrates the builder's unwavering passion for energy conservation and use of solar energy technology. It is the 2006 EnergyValue Housing Award gold winner in the Custom Home, Moderate Climate category. This home was also chosen as NAHB's 2007 Green Building Project of the Year. Credit: NAHB Research Center.

Ferrier Custom Homes of Fort Worth, Texas, NAHB's 2007 Green Builder Advocate of the Year, built this home. It won the 2007 EnergyValue Housing Award gold award in the category of Custom Home and Hot Climate. Features include sustainable materials, near-zero energy consumption, and a solar water heating system. Credit: NAHB Research Center.

U.S. Green Building Council

The U.S. Green Building Council (USGBC) is excited to be a first-time sponsor of the 2007 Solar Decathlon. With a wealth of industry experience in green building, the USGBC, a nonprofit organization composed of leaders from across the building industry, is looking forward to working with tomorrow's builders, architects, and designers to advance the industry toward building environmentally responsible, profitable, and healthy spaces in which to live and work.

Since its founding in 1993, USGBC has focused on fulfilling the building and construction industry's vision for its own transformation to high-performance green building. Today, it includes more than 11,000 member companies and organizations. In the past five years alone, USGBC's membership has quadrupled, and more than 2 billion square feet of building space are involved with its Leadership in Energy and Environmental Design (LEED) program.

The Council is as diverse as the marketplace it serves. Membership includes building owners and end-users, real estate developers, architects, engineers, students, and educators. Driving its mission to transform the built environment is the LEED Green Building Rating System, which is accessible online and supported by a robust LEED Workshop program, and the LEED Professional Accreditation program. USGBC supports a rich education and research agenda, including Greenbuild — the largest international conference and expo focused on green building.

LEED is a voluntary building-certification program that defines high-performance green buildings, which are healthier, and more environmentally responsible and profitable structures. LEED addresses a variety of buildings and building-project types through individualized systems, including new construction, existing buildings, commercial interiors, core and shell, homes, and neighborhood development.

The LEED for Homes program is a voluntary rating system that promotes the design and construction of high-performance "green" homes. A green home uses less energy, water, and natural resources; creates less waste; and is healthier and more comfortable for the occupants. Benefits of a LEED home include lower energy and water bills; reduced greenhouse gas emissions; and less exposure to mold, mildew, and other indoor toxins. USGBC began the pilot test of the LEED for Homes program in August 2005. More than 400 builders representing 7,500 homes across the United States are participating in the pilot program, and more than 200 homes have been LEED certified. The pilot test will conclude in fall 2007, and USGBC will launch the LEED for Homes program rating system after member approval in November.

With its commitment to increasing knowledge of, and expertise in, sustainable building, USGBC is proud to support the Solar Decathlon. ♦

A cornerstone of the U.S. Green Building Council's mission to transform the built environment is its Leadership in Energy and Environmental Design program, which promotes and recognizes the development of high-performance green buildings such as the ones shown here.

Credit: SpawGlass

Credit: Heather Ferrier

Credit: M-Buck Studio, LLC

BP

Once again, BP is proud to be a title sponsor of the 2007 Solar Decathlon. Events such as the Solar Decathlon offer BP an opportunity to provide support to some of the finest international academic teams exploring today's and tomorrow's practical application of solar power. As in previous Decathlon competitions, BP Solar is offering the teams discounted solar materials and technological advice.

As one of the world's largest energy companies, BP is committed to making solar power a more affordable and accessible part of everyday life. With solar electricity being used increasingly by home and business owners to reduce electric bills, the designs created by the Solar Decathlon teams often contain many economical options for today's marketplace. Already throughout Europe and the Americas, BP Solar offers a clean energy option to supplement or replace utility power.

In late 2005, BP launched BP Alternative Energy, a low-carbon power business focusing on solar, wind, hydrogen power, and gas-fired power. BP Solar, which has been in business for more than 30 years, is a key business within BP Alternative Energy and a global company with more than 2,200 employees focused on harnessing the sun's energy to produce solar electricity. BP Solar leads the industry by providing progressively efficient and cost-effective solar electric systems to international markets. This includes the design, manufacture, and marketing of quality solar electric systems for a wide range of applications in the residential, commercial, and industrial sectors.

BP Solar is one of the world's largest solar companies and has manufacturing facilities in the United States, Spain, India, and Australia. In remote areas such as the Philippines, BP Solar is bringing solar power to more than 400,000 residents in 150 remote villages. In the United States, in partnership with the Enterprise Foundation and the Environmental Media Association, the BP Solar Neighbors program provides solar electric systems to low-income families in Southern California whenever a celebrity purchases a solar system.

These activities, together with our involvement in the Solar Decathlon, exemplify the values that drive BP — innovation, high-quality performance, a progressive and better way of doing things, and a commitment to environmental and community leadership. We invest in science, education, and technology to help achieve a sustainable future and brighter tomorrow. ♦

The PV system on this home in Danville, California, consists of 48 BP Solar EnergyTile modules that comprise a 3.1-kW system. This home is part of the Ponderosa community. Credit: BP

The BP Solar manufacturing facility and international headquarters located in Frederick, Maryland, is the largest fully integrated PV manufacturing plant in the United States. Credit: BP

SPRINT NEXTEL

Sprint Nextel is honored and excited to be a part of the 2007 Solar Decathlon by providing secure high-speed, wireless Internet access to the teams competing. The innovation demonstrated by teams participating in the Solar Decathlon taps into another important goal of ours — preserving the environment. From researching renewable power to recycling used cell phones, Sprint Nextel demonstrates its commitment to the environment everyday.

In our daily business activities, we actively pursue the use of renewable power technologies to better serve our customers. Telecommunications facilities rely heavily on commercial power to run their networks. However, overhead utility lines and outdoor substations are subject to both human and natural forces (such as tornadoes and lightning) that can shut down telecommunications. For this reason, back-up power sources are needed. The most commonly used forms of back-up power, such as lead-acid batteries and diesel generators, have drawbacks — noise, leakage, or polluting exhaust.

Sprint Nextel has researched several alternative power technologies that provide many benefits to the environment, including significantly reduced noise levels and pollutants. For example, one of these technologies, fuel cells, releases no pollutants. The fuel cell's only exhaust is drinkable water, which is endorsed by the U.S. Environmental Protection Agency. Solar power is also being field-trialed at small communication sites as a way to reduce utility costs by minimizing grid usage during daylight hours.

Sprint Nextel is interested in alternative power technologies because they provide benefits to the environment and can be combined with other technologies to improve the performance of our network, which means more reliable service for our customers. As we continue to provide new and enhanced wireless applications and services, uninterrupted telecom service — both on cell phones and for wireless Internet access — becomes even more critical. At Sprint, our goal is to provide the best quality network through the use of cleaner, more efficient technology.

Sprint Wireless Recycling

Wireless recycling is an important part of Sprint Nextel's environmental commitment. In 2001, we created Sprint Project Connect, a wireless-phone recycling program that has prevented millions of phones from ending up in landfills.

Sprint Project Connect accepts all makes and models of phones, regardless of service provider. To recycle your phone, pick up a postage-paid envelope at any participating Sprint store nationwide. Or, print the postage-paid mailing label available on the Project Connect Web site (www.sprint.com/citizenship/communities_across/project_connect.html).

Since 2001, Sprint has collected nearly 7 million used wireless phones and kept those phones out of the waste stream through Sprint Project Connect and other separate equipment collection efforts such as Sprint Buyback, a program that gives Sprint customers account credit for returning eligible, no-longer-used phones. The phones are either recycled or refurbished and resold.

Net proceeds from Sprint Project Connect go to benefit kindergarten through 12th-grade education programs. Since its inception, the project has raised more than $3 million for charitable programs. ♦

Sprint Nextel provided the 2005 Solar Decathlon homes with high-speed, wireless Internet access and is doing the same for the 2007 Decathlon. Credit: Stefano Paltera

BLUE EGG

Blue Egg is an e-media company that celebrates attainable sustainable living. Through our Web sites, we provide clear, credible information and practical solutions to help people become more mindful of the environment — without suggesting they surrender style, comfort, and convenience, and without asking them to spend a lot of extra cash. We support and applaud the 2007 Solar Decathletes and the important work they are doing. We are honored to be part of this international event that delivers a clear message of hope and virtually unlimited possibilities for today and tomorrow.

Blue Egg's Web sites offer solid information, vital context, and straightforward advice from a variety of experts. Our unique online tools can help everyone, from newbie to eco-veteran, discover new ways to live without taking a toll on the planet. Blue Egg's first site, Green Building Blocks, was launched in November 2006; it is already the largest online resource for residential green building and remodeling. Green Building Blocks features more than 1,500 environmentally friendly products, a national directory of 2,900 green-building professionals, case studies, how-tos, and much more. Blue Egg built upon the Green Building Blocks Web site to create the Solar Decathlon product directory, which lists the products used by the Decathletes in their projects. We encourage you to meet the teams, experience their houses, and visit the product directory to learn first-hand what you can do to live more sustainably. ◆

www.blueegg.com
www.greenbuildingblocks.com

With each Solar Decathlon, the list of sponsors wanting to participate and contribute has grown. A strong motivation is the desire to create a better world for children such as these, who visited the Decathlon in 2005.

HONEYWELL

Honeywell is proud to be part of the 2007 Solar Decathlon competition and supports its goal of building and operating the most attractive and energy-efficient solar-powered home. This unique international event is aligned with Honeywell's own mission, which includes building a world that is more comfortable and energy efficient.

As a first-time supporting sponsor, Honeywell is offering participants its non-ozone-depleting blowing agent used in foam insulation, as well as touchscreen programmable thermostats and other comfort controls and technologies. All of these play an important role in improving energy efficiency and lowering heating and cooling costs for homeowners worldwide.

Honeywell's Enovate blowing agent is the main factor in determining insulation performance, or R-value, in closed-cell polyurethane spray foam insulation used in walls and roofing. This energy-efficient technology, used for many years to help appliances achieve ENERGY STAR ratings, is rapidly being adopted to insulate homes, as well as in novel applications such as insulating solar water heaters in China and hurricane-proofing commercial facilities such as the Louisiana Superdome.

As part of its sponsorship, Honeywell also is providing shirts, jackets, and accessories for organizers, volunteers, students, and other personnel who will gather at the National Mall in Washington, D.C.

As demand for energy continues to rise, Honeywell is committed to helping homeowners maximize energy efficiency and reduce heating and cooling costs. We at Honeywell wish all participants the best of luck in the 2007 Solar Decathlon. ◆

www.honeywell.com

THANKS TO SO MANY

The Solar Decathlon would not be possible without the generous support of so many people. We are grateful to the sponsors listed in the preceding pages — and to those listed below. We also acknowledge the volunteers, technical experts, and in-kind contributors whose support is vital to making the Solar Decathlon an enriching experience for the teams and spectators alike.

United States Department of Agriculture (USDA)
www.usda.gov
The USDA supports the goals of the Solar Decathlon and is pleased to be participating in the event.

Midwest Research Institute (MRI)
www.mriresearch.org
MRI is generously sponsoring the Victory Reception at the end of the Solar Decathlon, which gives the student competitors a chance to celebrate their achievements and applaud each other.

International Code Council (ICC)
www.iccsafe.org
ICC generously discounted 22 copies of the 2006 International Codes on CD Complete Collection.

The National Fire Protection Agency (NFPA)
www.nfpa.org
NFPA donated 22 CD-ROMs of the 2005 National Electric Code Handbook for use by Solar Decathlon teams and organizers.

CertainTeed Corporation
www.certainteed.com
CertainTeed is sponsoring a lunch during the Decathlon for all of the student competitors.

HON
www.hon.com
HON is providing furniture for the main tent, the team lounge, and several teams.

Orange Element Design
www.orange-element.com
Orange Element helped to develop and is hosting the MySpace page for the Decathlon competitors.

Owens Corning
www.owenscorning.com
Owens Corning sponsored printing of the Energy Savers booklet, which is being distributed to the public.

Reluminati
www.reluminati.com
Reluminati is providing a renewable power source for the Anatomy of a House exhibit.

Texas Instruments (TI)
www.ti.com
TI is sponsoring the work of Jim Tetro, a photographer who is taking architectural-style photos of all the team houses for use by Decathlon organizers and sponsors.

Xantrex
www.xantrex.com
Xantrex is providing a lunch for the Decathlon competitors.

Solar Decathlon Web Links

Solar Decathlon Blog
eere.typepad.com/solar_decathlon
This site gives you the visitor — and the competitors, organizers, and sponsors — an opportunity to post comments and insights about the Solar Decathlon. It also features a journal by Richard King, the director of the competition, with on-the-scene coverage of the daily happenings during the 2007 Solar Decathlon.

Solar Decathlon MySpace Page
www.myspace.com/solardecathlon07
Here's another chance to post comments or just to read what others have to say. The page also has links to information and resources on topics such as sustainable building practices and solar energy incentives and tax credits.

Solar Decathlon Product Directory
www.greenbuildingblocks.com/solar_decathlon.go
Want to know where the competitors get the products you see in their houses? Visit this page to find out about the solar technologies, appliances, windows, lighting, and many other products used in the Decathlon houses.